TEXTS
FROM
THE BUDDHIST CANON

TEXTS
FROM
THE BUDDHIST CANON,

COMMONLY KNOWN AS

DHAMMAPADA,

WITH ACCOMPANYING NARRATIVES.

Translated from the Chinese

BY

SAMUEL BEAL

(B.A. TRIN. COLL. CAMB)
PROFESSOR OF CHINESE, UNIVERSITY COLLEGE,
LONDON

GYAN

Published by

GYAN

Gyan Publishing House
5, Ansari Road
Daryaganj, New Delhi-110002
Phone: 011-47034999, 9811692060
E-mail: books@gyanbooks.com

Distribution Network
gyanbooks.com
India, USA, Canada, UK, Australia, France

ISBN : 978-81-212-2512-0 (HB)
First Published, 1878

2nd Impression 2021

Printed at: Gyan Press, Delhi.

Texts from the Buddhist Canon
Author: Samuel Beal

TEXTS

FROM

THE BUDDHIST CANON,

COMMONLY KNOWN AS

DHAMMAPADA,

WITH ACCOMPANYING NARRATIVES.

Translated from the Chinese

BY

SAMUEL BEAL

(B.A. TRIN. COLL. CAMB.)

PROFESSOR OF CHINESE, UNIVERSITY COLLEGE, LONDON.

LONDON:

TRÜBNER & CO., LUDGATE HILL.

1878.

DEDICATED

TO

HIS EXCELLENCY, IWAKURA TOMOMI,

IN RECOGNITION OF HIS LIBERALITY

IN PROCURING FOR THE LIBRARY OF THE INDIA OFFICE

A COMPLETE COPY OF THE BUDDHIST TRIPIṬAKA

IN THE CHINESE LANGUAGE, FROM ONE VOLUME OF WHICH

The following Translation

HAS BEEN PREPARED.

CONTENTS.

*** [In the section No. XXXI. will be found the sermon preached by Buddha to his son Râhula on "Falsehood." This sermon or exhortation is alluded to by Aṣoka in the Edict of Bhabra.]

INTRODUCTORY REMARKS.

DHAMMAPADA (which, according to the Chinese Gloss, may be rendered "Scriptural Texts" or "Verses") is a work of much importance in the study of Buddhism. It contains, as its title signifies, authentic Texts gathered from ancient canonical books—and these Texts are generally connected with some incident or other in the History of Buddha, helping to illustrate everyday life in India at the time when they were written, as well as the method of teaching adopted by the Founder of this remarkable Religion. Not only does the general tone pervading these verses illustrate the spirit of Buddha's doctrine,[1] but by a critical examination of particular passages, we are enabled to solve some of the difficulties which always attend the interpretation of words and phrases used in a religious sense. We already possess two translations of this work from the Pâli,—one by V. Fausböll (1855), the other by Max Müller (1870)[2]—and in addition to these there are the criticisms of Mr. James D'Alwis and the late Professor Childers on the latter translation—so that for all necessary purposes we have

[1] Mr. Spence Hardy has observed that a collection might be made from the precepts of this work, that in the purity of its ethics could scarcely be equalled from any other heathen author.—"Eastern Monachism," 169

[2] Mr. Gogerly has also translated 350 verses of Dhammapada (out of 423).—Spence Hardy, "E. M." p. 28. [A. Weber's German translation appeared in 1860.]

sufficient material before us for a correct knowledge of the work in question. I should not under these circumstances have undertaken to produce another translation bearing the same title, but for the fact that no copy of Dhammapada has hitherto been known to exist in China. It has been my good fortune to have had brought under my immediate examination the great body of books comprising the Chinese Buddhist Canon. Amongst these I found there were four copies of a work bearing the title of "Law verses" or "Scriptural texts," which on examination were seen to resemble the Pâli version of Dhammapada in many particulars. Supposing that some knowledge of these books would be acceptable to the student, I have undertaken the translation[1] of the simplest of them, and with such notices of the other copies as are suggested by a brief comparison of them one with the other, I now offer my book for candid consideration.

[1] It may here be stated, in order to disarm unfriendly criticism, that I do not profess to have produced a literal translation of the Chinese Text, but only such an abstract of it as seemed necessary for my purpose.

PREFACE

TO THE

CHINESE VERSION OF DHAMMAPADA.

THERE are four principal copies of Dhammapada in Chinese. The first, approaching most nearly to the Pâli, was made by a Shaman "Wei-chi-lan" (and others), who lived during the Wu dynasty, about the beginning of the third century of the Christian era. As this is the earliest version, we will consider it first.

The title by which it is known is *Fa-kheu-King*,[1] that is, "The Sûtra of Law Verses." The symbol *kheu* (句) does not necessarily mean "a verse," but is applied to any sentence or phrase: the rendering "Law texts" or "Scripture texts" would therefore be more correct were it not that in the Preface to this work the symbol is explained by "Gâthâ," which is stated by Childers (*sub voce*) to mean "a verse or stanza," or generally "a çloka or anushṭubh stanza." Nothing can be more precise than the language of the Chinese Preface (to which I have alluded in the "Report on the Catalogue of the Chinese Tripiṭaka," p. 113), in which it is stated that the work we are considering is the "Tan-po-këĕ," 曇鉢偈, which can only be restored to Dharmagâthâpadaṁ, and as gâthâpadam is used for "a stanza," we come back to the meaning of "Scripture, or Law-

[1] In the *Encyclopædia* "Chi-yuen-fă-pao-khân-tung-tsung-lu" (Kiouen xi. fol. $\frac{21}{1}$), this work is also quoted as "Fă-tsah," *i.e.*, "Scriptural Miscellanies."

stanzas." Of course, the Chinese affords no assistance in solving the question "whether 'pada,' in the singular, can ever mean a collection of verses,"[1] and the other difficulties attaching to the correct rendering of this word from the Pâli; but as an independent testimony to the sense of the expression "Dhammapada," as it was understood by the old translators in China, it may be of value.[2] The Preface further explains that these verses are "choice selections from all the Sûtras," which agrees with what we know from actual comparison, as also from the testimony of independent writers.[3] The Chinese Sûtras, *e.g.*, contain many passages found in Dhammapada—compare the following, p. 49: "As the bee collects nectar and departs without injuring the flower or its colour and scent, so let the sage dwell upon earth," with *Catena*, p. 150, "As the butterfly alights on the flower and destroys not its form or its sweetness, but takes a sip and then departs, so the mendicant follower of Buddha (sage) takes not nor hurts another's possessions." And the stanza following this (No. 50) is but a part of the same traditional record as coming from a former Buddha (*Wessabha*): "Not the failure of others, nor their sins of commission or omission, but his own misdeeds and negligences should the sage take notice of." So in the Chinese: "He observes not another man's actions or omissions, looks only to his own behaviour and conduct." (*Op. cit.*, p. 159.) Again, let us compare v. 183 with the Chinese record of Konagamana Buddha (*Catena*, 159),

[1] But we must remember the remark of the translator of "Sutta Nipáta," that in old Pâli works the singular is frequently used for the plural.—"Sutta Nipáta," by Sir N. Coomára Swami. Introd. xix. (Trübner & Co.)

[2] It may be as well to state, however, that the word "pada" is in various compounds rendered by "traces," or "*vestigia*," in the Chinese, such, for example, as in the word "Karipadadeva" (*elephantis vestigia habens deus.*—"Jul. Méthode," p. 71), where "pada" is equal to the Chinese "tsi," which means "a trace," or, "footstep." (For other examples, *vide* the Chinese version of the "Lotus," compared with that by Burnouf, p. 155. Also "Jul. Hiouen Thsang," iii. p. 498, &c.)

[3] Mr. James D'Alwis, for example, in his "Review of Max Müller's Dhammapada," pp. 92, 93, ss., and elsewhere.

"Not to commit any sin, to do good, and to purify one's mind, this is the teaching of the Awakened;" the Chinese is, "Practising no evil way, advancing in the exercise of virtue, purifying both mind and will, this is the doctrine of all the Buddhas." Again, stanza 214 in the Pâli is this, "From lust comes grief, from lust comes fear, he who is free from lust knows neither grief nor fear." This is evidently the same as the testimony of Kâsyapa Buddha, "A man from lust engenders sorrow, and from sorrow guilty fear; banish lust and there will be no sorrow, and if no sorrow then no guilty fear." (*Catena*, p. 200.) Without quoting further at length, we will simply note a few other agreements, *e.g.*, compare stanza 239 with *Catena*, p. 201, § 34; stanza 281 with the record of Kâsyapa (*Catena*, 159); stanza 292 with p. 264 (*op. cit.*); stanza 372 with p. 247 (*op. cit.*); and in many other cases. But perhaps the most curious agreement is to be found in various stanzas which occur in the Chinese version of the "Lankâvatâra Sûtra," which was translated into Chinese by a priest Gunabhadra, early in the Sung dynasty (*Circ.* 420 A.D.). Of these I shall only select one as throwing some light on a difficult verse in the Pâli; I refer to vv. 294, 295, which run thus: "A true Brahmana, though he has killed father and mother and two valiant kings, though he has destroyed a kingdom with all its subjects, is free from guilt."

"A true Brahmana, though he has killed father and mother and two holy kings, and even a fifth man, is free from guilt."

With respect to these verses, both Professor Max Müller and Professor Childers are inclined to regard them as showing that a truly holy man who commits such sins as those specified is nevertheless guiltless. But in the third book, p. 3, of the "Lankâvatâra Sûtra" we find the following exposition of this doctrine:—"At this time Mahâmati Bodhisatwa addressed Buddha and said, 'According to the assertion of the Great Teacher, if a male or female disciple should commit either of the unpardonable sins, he or she, nevertheless, shall not be cast into hell. World-honoured One! how can this be, that such a disciple shall escape though guilty of such sins?' To whom Buddha replied, 'Mahâmati! attend, and weigh my words well! . . . . What are these five unpardonable sins of which you speak? They are these, to slay father or mother, to wound a Rahat, to offend (*i.e.*, to place a stumbling-block in the way of) the members of the sañgha (church), to draw the blood from the body of a Buddha. Mahâmati! say, then, how a man committing these sins can be guiltless? In this way;—is not Love (*Taṇhâ*) which covets pleasure more and more, and so produces 'birth'—is not this the mother (*mâtâ*) of all? And is not 'ignorance' (*avidyâ*) the father (*pitâ*) of all? To destroy these two, then, is to slay father and mother. And again, to cut off and destroy those ten '*kleshas*' (Ch. *shi*) which like the rat, or the secret poison, work invisibly, and to get rid of all the consequences of these faults (*i.e.*, to destroy all material associations), this is to wound a Rahat. And so to cause offence and overthrow a church or assembly, what is this but to separate entirely the connection of the five *skandhas*? ('five *aggregates*,' which is the same word as that used above for the 'Church.') And again, to draw the blood of a Buddha, what is this but to wound and get rid of the seven-fold body by the three methods of escape. (The seven-fold body, literally 'the body with seven kinds of knowledge'—the number *seven* in this connection evidently runs parallel with the *seven* Buddhas, whose blood is supposed to be spilt; the three methods of escape are the same as the three 'yânas,' or vehicles; viz., Srâvakas, Bodhisatwas, Buddhas). Thus it is, Mahâmati, the holy male or female disciple may slay father and mother, wound a Rahat, overthrow the assembly, draw the blood of Buddha, and yet escape the punishment of the lowest hell (*avîchi*). And in order to explain and enforce this more fully, the World-honoured One added the following stanzas :—

> 'Lust, or carnal desire, this is the Mother,
> "Ignorance," this is the Father,
> The highest point of knowledge, this is Buddha,
> All the "Kleshas" these are the Rahats,
> The five Skandhas, these are the Priests,
> To commit the five unpardonable sins
> Is to destroy these five
> And yet not suffer the pains of hell.'"

These comparisons will be sufficient to show the plan of the work under consideration, and to confirm the statement of the writer of the preface, "that these stanzas are but choice selections from the various Sûtras."[1] We shall now understand the remark that "there are various arrangements or editions of the Dhammapada" (Chinese Preface), for it seems plain that these selections from the canonical books were not made at any one time, or generally accepted in their present form, until a much later period than the compilation of the Sûtras themselves. The language of the Preface is equally distinct on this point, "It was from these works, viz., the Canonical Scriptures, that the Shamans in *after ages* copied out various Gâthâs, some of four lines, and some of six lines,[2] and attached to each set of verses a title according to the subject therein explained." We may thus account for the various editions of the work which exist in China, compiled from original versions in India, shewing that there existed in that country also not one, but several copies of these "excerpta." We must accept Dhammapada then in its present form, simply as a redaction made at an early period from canonical books, for the purpose of ready reference, or as a religious "*vade-mecum.*"

[1] Which Sûtras form the second of the three baskets of the Buddhist Canon.

[2] These lines probably correspond to those named by Spence Hardy,—(*Eastern Monach*, p. 28).

The Chinese copies of this work, without exception, refer its first arrangement to the venerable Dharmatrâta[1] (vid. *Julien*, sub voce Fă-kieou, iii. p. 441). The difficulty is to find out when Dharmatrâta lived. He was certainly the author of the Samyuktâbhidharma Shaster —but although the Chinese version of this book is before me, it gives no clue to the time in which its author flourished. Burnouf (Introduction, pp. 566, 567) alludes to the Sthavira Dharmatrâta, otherwise Bhadanta Dharmatrâta, as one of the most illustrious of the earliest Apostles of Buddhism. But there is much confusion in the whole matter. Whether Sthavira Dharmatrâta is a different personage from Bhadanta Dharmatrâta, and when either of them lived is not explained. Suffice it to say, that the author of Dhammapada is all along spoken of in our Chinese books as "Tsun-che-fă-kieou," that is, Ârya Dharmatrâta, and in the preface to the "Ch'uh-yau-king" he is said to have been the uncle of "Po-su-meh," *i.e.*, Vasumitra. If this patriarch be the one "who took a principal part in the last revision of the Canon, as the President of the Synod under Kanishka" (Eitel, sub voce, *Vasumitra*), then we have fair ground for assigning him an approximate date. Kanishka we assume to have reigned about 40 B.C., and if so, then Dharmatrâta may with much probability be placed some thirty years earlier—or about 70 B.C.

The question to be considered now is whether it is likely that a book compiled at this date would have gained such authority as to be accepted as semi-canonical by the numerous translators who flocked to China some two or three hundred years afterwards. (We dismiss for the present the consideration of the relation of this work to that known in the South.) Considering the wonderful

[1] According to Târanâtha, Dharmatrâta was cotemporary with the Brahman Râhula; he, with Ghoshaka, Vasumitra, and Buddhadeva, were the four great Âchâryas of the Vaibhâshikas. He distinguishes this Bhadanta Dh. from another Dh., who collected the Udânavarga. (Schiefner's German transl., p. 68.)

impetus given to Buddhist research at the time alluded to, there can be no difficulty in accepting this position. The writings of Asaṅgha, Vasubandhu, Nâgârjuna, Vasumitra, and others who lived during the first century B.C., are accepted in the Northern School of Buddhism as authoritative. They have just that weight and character which works written by those called "Fathers of the Christian Church" have in Christendom. In the Chinese Tripiṭaka there is no effort to conceal the human composition of these books. On the title page of every Shaster the author's name is given—they are called "Sûtras" or "Shasters"—but yet with the plain intimation that they were drawn up by men who lived long after the age of what we should call "inspiration." If, then, these other writers are regarded with reverence, equally so we may assume was the author of the present work. In any case it is of importance that we have here provided for us a definite assertion as to Dhammapada, with respect to its date and author—about which the Southern Records, beyond the general assignation of this work to a portion of the canon, affirm nothing.

It now remains to consider what reliance may be placed generally on these Chinese versions of the Sacred Books of the Buddhists. At the very outset of this consideration we observe that they were made, if not by, yet under the immediate direction of, Indian priests. It would be as incorrect to refer the originals of the Christian Scriptures now used in China to native writers, as to make the Buddhist books found there a part of the native literature. Buddhism was brought to China by missionaries from India, and the books forming the canon (except where expressly named as Chinese) are translations made by those men from some Indian vernacular. This leads to another remark in correction of an oft-repeated assertion that Chinese Buddhist books are all translations of *Sanscrit* works found in Nipal. It is so plain to any one conversant with the subject that such is not the case, that any lengthened remarks on the point seem to be unnecessary. We have already in English a translation of the Pâtimokkham̃, or, as it is known in Sanscrit, the Prâtimoksha, from the Chinese; and this version is found to agree accurately (except in some additions of a later date) with the translation from the Pâli by Mr. Gogerly. Then again, we have the Samajâtaka in Chinese, agreeing in the main with the Pâli; the Brahmajâla Sûtra (Case lxxvii. *Catalogue*); the Parinirvâna Sûtra (do.); the Sigâlovâda (do.); the Sârdûla Karna Sûtra (Case xxxii.), and many others, which from internal evidence we may certainly conclude were not translated from Sanscrit. And that this is so, is corroborated by the fact that many of the Buddhist books known in China were brought immediately to that country from Ceylon by Fa-hien, and translated into Chinese directly from the sacred language of that country. But before the time of Fa-hien there had been a continuous migration of Indian priests into China, who brought with them books from Northern and Central India, written, therefore, in the dialects of those countries, and which were from them carefully translated.[1] These remarks will be sufficient to correct the mistake alluded to without going into further particulars. Nor would even so much have been necessary if the statements as to the character of Chinese Buddhist translations had not been endorsed by some leading scholars of the time. Take, for example, the remark of Professor Childers ("Contemporary Review," February 1876), that "the Northern books (so-called), [which of course include the Chinese,] are of as little value for a critical examination of Buddhism, as works found in Abyssinia bearing on the Christian religion would be for an exact acquaintance with Christianity." It is plain, however, that the Buddhist works in China are of great value for an exact knowledge of that religion, because

[1] In the present work we have the forms, "Gijjhakûṭo," "Râjagaha," "Sâvatthî," &c., to represent the Sanscrit, "Gṛidhrakûta," "Râjagṛiha," "Śrâvastî," &c.

they are faithful versions of works everywhere known in India, not only during the early period of its history, but also throughout its development—or, to put it into plain figures, the books found in China afford us a consecutive catena of writings dating from at least 100 B.C. to 600 A.D., that is, during a period of 700 years. More than this can scarcely be desired for a perfect study of any religious system.

We come now to a comparison of this earliest translation with that from the Pâli. The Fă-kheu-king contains thirty-nine chapters against the twenty-six of the Southern edition, and 760[1] stanzas against 423. We are told, however, in the preface that the original work consisted of twenty-six chapters and 500 stanzas; and as in Buddhist calculations the next highest round number is frequently used to denote the exact number intended, we have in this statement sufficient evidence to show that the original from which our translation was made consisted of the same chapters, and probably the same number of verses, as that known in the South—in other words, that they were identical. If so, the question arises, *Who* added the thirteen additional sections? It would appear from the wording of the preface that this was the work of the Indian missionary (or refugee) Tsiang-im, who added these sections after due consultation [*tsze wan*], taking care to verify them from ancient sources. If this be so (the passage is confessedly obscure), it would lead us to suppose that the original manuscript brought to China was the same as that known in Ceylon, the differences which occur between the two being attributable to special reasons existing at the time of the translation.

[1] In the preface it is stated that there are only 752 stanzas. The difference between this and the sum of the headings of each chapter must be accidental. It is curious that a similar discrepancy occurs in the Pâli summary of stanzas—there are *five* verses more in the text than in the index in that version, and in the Chinese *eight* more (*Vide* Max Müller's Dh. ix. n.)

I will now proceed to give a tabular statement of the chapters and verses which compose the Chinese and Pâli versions respectively, so as to render a comparison of the two easy:—

CHINESE. *Title of Chapter.*	No. of Verses.	PÂLI. *Title of Chapter.*	No. of Verses.
1. Impermanence	21		
2. Inciting to Wisdom	29		
3. The Srâvaka	19		
4. Simple Faith	18		
5. Observance of Duty	16		
6. Reflection	12		
7. Loving Kindness	19		
8. Conversation	12		
9. Twin Verses	22	1. Twin Verses	20
10. Carelessness	20	2. Reflection	12
11. Thought	12	3. Thought	11
12. Flowers	17	4. Flowers	16
13. The Fool	21	5. The Fool	16
14. The Wise Man	17	6. The Wise Man	14
15. The Rahat	10	7. The Venerable	10
16. The Thousands	16	8. The Thousands	16
17. Evil Conduct	22	9. Evil	13
18. Punishment	14	10. Punishment	17
19. Old Age	14	11. Old Age	11
20. Self Love	14	12. Self	10
21. The World	14	13. The World	12
22. Buddha	21	14. The Awakened	18
23. Rest and Repose	14	15. Happiness	12
24. Pleasure	12	16. Pleasure	12
25. Anger	26	17. Anger	14
26. Impurity	19	18. Impurity	21
27. Holding to the Law	17	19. The Just	17
28. The Way	28	20. The Way	17
29. Miscellaneous	14	21. Miscellaneous	16
30. Hell	16	22. The Backward Course	14
31. The Elephant	18	23. The Elephant	14
32. Lust	32	24. Thirst	26
33. Advantageous Service	20	[Absent]	
34. The Shaman	32	25. The Bhikshu	23
35. The Brahmachârin	40	26. The Brâhmana	41
36. Nirvâna	36		
37. Birth and Death	18		
38. Profit of Religion	19		
39. Good Fortune	19		

We see, then, that from the ninth chapter to the thirty-fifth (with one exception, viz., the thirty-third) the two works contain the same succession of subjects, whilst there are seventy-nine more stanzas in the Chinese than in the Pâli throughout the chapters common to each. We may reasonably gather from the entire consideration that the version of Dhammapada by Dharmatrâta, which was brought to China by Wei-chi-lan, was itself a recension of an earlier edition of the same work known in India—that Dharmatrâta, whilst retaining the number of chapters and their subjects of consideration, added some additional stanzas to them, and that this work so revised or re-edited, was accepted by the Council held under the presidency of his nephew Vasumitra, during the reign of Kanishka, and thus acquired the reputation of a canonical portion of the Tripiṭaka.[1] If, however, the additions made to the number of stanzas in the different chapters can be referred to the Chinese editors (themselves Indians), then we may argue that the copies of Dhammapada, known in the north and south, may both be compilations of Dharmatrâta, and that he was the first to draw up this collection of texts and to give it (from his own personal authority) the character of a canonical book.

With respect to the accuracy of the Chinese version, it will be plain to every Chinese scholar from the following passage, that entire reliance may be placed on it. I will select the twenty-fifth chapter of the Pâli and the thirty-fourth of the Chinese for comparison: the former contains twenty-three stanzas, the latter thirty-two. The title in the one case is "The Shaman," in the other "The Bhikshu":

[1] There are some references to Dharmatrâta in M. Wassilief's work on "Buddhism" (le Bouddisme, Paris, 1865) viz., in §§ 48, 50, 270. From these it would seem that he was one of the great leaders of the Vaibhâshikas. It would not be surprising if we found that the edition of Dhammapada prepared by Dharmatrâta, belonged to the Vaibhâshika school, whilst that known in Ceylon was compiled by the Sautrântikas.

沙門品

端目耳鼻口 身意常守正 比丘行如是

可以免衆苦 手足莫妄犯 節言愼所行

常內樂定意 守一行寂然

學當守口 寡言安徐 法義爲定 言必柔輭

樂法欲法 思惟安法 比丘依法 正而不費

學無求利 無愛他行 比丘好他 不得定意

比丘少取 以得無積 天人所譽 生淨無穢

比丘爲慈 愛敬佛敎 深入止觀 滅行乃安

一切名色
比丘扈船
捨五斷五
禪無放逸
無禪不智
當學入空
當制五陰
不受所有
生當行淨
如衛師華

非有莫惑
中虛則輕
思惟五根
莫為欲亂
無智不禪
靜居止意
伏意如水
為慧比丘
求善師友
勉知自墮

不近不憂
除婬怒癡
能分別五
無吞鎔銅
道從禪智
樂獨屏處
清淨和悅
攝根知足
智者成人
釋婬怒癡

乃為比丘
是為泥洹
乃度河淵
自惱燋形
得至泥洹
一心觀法
為甘露味
戒律悉持
度苦致喜
生死自解

正身正言
當自飭身
我自為我
喜在佛教
儻有少行
棄慢無餘
知是勝於
比丘渡河
截流自忖
為之為之

心守玄默
內與心爭
計無有我
可以多喜
應佛教誡
驕　蓮華水
故　割愛無
流　勝欲明
折心却欲
必強自制

比丘棄世
護身念諦
故當損我
至到寂寞
此照世間
生淨　學能
戀慕　不受
於故
入不割欲
捨家而懈

是為受寂
比丘惟安
調乃為賢
行滅水安
如日無曀*
捨彼此
如蓮華
一意猶走
意猶復染

---

* Here ends the Text as found in the Pâli. I have, however, added the whole of the Chinese.

行懈緩者
沙門何行
袈裟披肩
不調難戒
息心非剔
息心非剔

勞意弗除
如意不禁
爲惡不損
如風枯樹
慢訑無戒
放逸無信

非淨梵行
步步著黏
行惡者死
自作爲身
捨貪思道
能滅衆苦

焉致大寶
但隨思走
斯墮惡道
易不精進
乃應息心
爲上沙門

TRANSLATION FROM THE PÂLI.

BY PROFESSOR MAX MÜLLER.

THE BHIKSHU (MENDICANT).

360.

Restraint in the eye is good, good is restraint in the ear, in the nose restraint is good, good is restraint in the tongue.

361.

In the body restraint is good, good is restraint in speech, in thought restraint is good, good is restraint in all things. A Bhikshu, restrained in all things, is freed from all pain.

362.

He who controls his hand, he who controls his feet, he who controls his speech, he who is well controlled, he who delights inwardly, who is collected, who is solitary and content, him they call Bhikshu.

363.

The Bhikshu who controls his mouth, who speaks wisely and calmly, who teaches the meaning and the Law, his word is sweet.

364.

He who dwells in the Law, delights in the Law, meditates on the Law, follows the Law, that Bhikshu will never fall away from the true Law.

365.

Let him not despise what he has received, nor ever envy others: a mendicant who envies others does not obtain peace of mind.

366.

A Bhikshu who, though he receives little, does not despise what he has received, even the gods will praise him, if his life is pure, and if he is not slothful.

367.

He who never identifies himself with his body and soul, and does not grieve over what is no more, he indeed is called a Bhikshu.

368.

The Bhikshu who acts with kindness, who is calm in the doctrine of Buddha, will reach the quiet place (Nirvâ*n*a), cessation of natural desires, and happiness.

369.

O Bhikshu, empty this boat! if emptied, it will go quickly; having cut off passion and hatred, thou wilt go to Nirvâ*n*a.

370.

Cut off the five (senses), leave the five, rise above the five? A Bhikshu, who has escaped from the five fetters, he is called Oghati*nn*a, "Saved from the flood."

371.

Meditate, O Bhikshu, and be not heedless! Do not direct thy thought to what gives pleasure! that thou mayest not for thy heedlessness have to swallow the iron ball (in hell), and that thou mayest not cry out when burning, "This is pain."

372.

Without knowledge there is no meditation, without meditation there is no knowledge; he who has knowledge and meditation is near unto Nirvâ*n*a.

373.

A Bhikshu who has entered his empty house, and whose mind is tranquil, feels a more than human delight when he sees the law clearly.

374.

As soon as he has considered the origin and destruction of the elements (khandha) of the body, he finds happiness and joy which belong to those who know the immortal (Nirvâ*n*a).

375.

And this is the beginning here for a wise Bhikshu: watchfulness over the senses, contentedness, restraint under the Law; keep noble friends whose life is pure, and who are not slothful.

376.

Let him live in charity, let him be perfect in his duties; then in the fulness of delight he will make an end of suffering.

377.

As the Vassikâ-plant sheds its withered flowers, men should shed passion and hatred, O ye Bhikshus!

378.

The Bhikshu whose body and tongue and mind are quieted, who is collected, and has rejected the baits of the world, he is called Quiet.

379.

Rouse thyself by thyself, examine thyself by thyself, thus self-protected and attentive wilt thou live happily, O Bhikshu!

380.

For self is the lord of self, self is the refuge of self; therefore curb thyself as the merchant curbs a good horse.

381.

The Bhikshu, full of delight, who is calm in the doctrine of Buddha, will reach the quiet place (Nirvâ*n*a), cessation of natural desires, and happiness.

382.

He who, even as a young Bhikshu, applies himself to the doctrine of Buddha, brightens up this world, like the moon when free from clouds.

After looking through this extract, we cannot doubt the fidelity of the Chinese version of Dhammapada,—and this section is only a fair sample of the whole.

This also helps to clear the way to a fair estimate of the value of Chinese Buddhist books generally.

The English version which follows is not made from the Text we have just considered, but from another about which I now proceed to speak. The "Fă-kheu-pi-ü,"[1]—*i.e.* parables connected with the book of scriptural texts—was translated by two Shamans of the western Tsin dynasty (A.D. 265 to A.D. 313). As its name denotes, it contains certain parables, or tales, connected with the verses which follow them, and which prompted their delivery. How far these tales are genuine may be difficult to determine. Professor Max Müller has already observed that

[1] In the "Chi-yuen-fă-pao-khàn-tung-tsung-lu," Kiouen x. fol. 1, this work is quoted as "Fa-kheu-pen-mih king," *i.e.*, "beginnings and endings from the book of scriptural texts" (Dhammapada), and it is explained in the margin that the verses are mere selections from the beginning and conclusion of the original work.

such stories "may have been invented to suit the text of the Dhammapada rather than *vice versâ*" (p. cvi. n.), and this appears to be very probable; but yet the stories found in the work before us must have been well known in India prior to the middle of the third century A.D., and judging from the ordinary period occupied in the transmission of such tales, we may reasonably refer them to a date perhaps as early as Dharmatrâta himself. The method adopted in this work is to give one or two tales, and a verse or more, as the Moral. The chapters are identical with the Fă-kheu-king—the only difference being that the verses or gâthas are fewer—they are, in fact, only a selection from the whole to meet the requirements of the story preceding them. This arrangement is in agreement with the original design of the work. Buddhaghosha, we are told, gives for each verse a parable to illustrate the meaning of the verse, and believed to have been uttered by Buddha in his intercourse with his disciples, or in preaching to the multitudes that came to hear him.[1] And so here we have a tale for each verse, delivered by Buddha for the benefit of his disciples, or others. As to the character of these stories, some of them are puerile and uninteresting. But if I mistake not, they are of a description not opposed to the character of the age to which they are assigned by the Chinese.

The method of teaching by parables, it is plain, was customary in India during the first and second centuries B.C. The Jâtakas, and the stories which occupy such a great part of the ordinary lives of Buddha (*vid.* Romantic Legend, *passim*), are illustrations of this. We know also from sculptures that these stories were familiar in India, and were, in fact, the ordinary means for instructing the people, at a date somewhere about the second century B.C., if not earlier,[2] so that I see no reason why the parables in this work, which was brought to China, in the first

[1] Max Müller, Dh. ix.

[2] The Sculptures at Bharahut are dated by General Cunningham from the time of Asoka, some 350 B.C.

instance, about 220 A.D, should not be the very ones attributed to Dharmatrâta at least 70 B.C. I am sorry that I have not been able to trace any agreement between these stories and those given by Buddhaghosha. Mr. Fausböll's notes are mostly mere transcriptions in Pâli, but yet enough may be gathered from these, even by one who is not a Pâli scholar, to make it clear that the stories to which he refers are not the same as those I have translated; the solution of this difficulty will have to be sought in the hint before alluded to, viz., that the parables were invented to suit the text of Dhammapada rather than *vice versâ* (Max Müller's Dh. cvi. n.). I shall leave any further observations on the Gâthâs which accompany the stories, for the notes that will be found in the book itself.

The third version of Dhammapada known in China is entitled "Chuh-yau-king," which may signify the Sûtra of "the Dawn," or "birth of Light."[1] This work is very much expanded, consisting, in fact, of seven volumes, comprising twenty *kiouen* or books. It is still referred to Ârya Dharmatrâta as its author; its translator was Chu-fo-nien (or, Fo-nien (Buddhasmriti?) the Indian (*Chu*) who lived during the Yaou-Tsin period, about 410 A.D. In the preface to this version we are told that Dharmatrâta was uncle of Vasumitra, and that he was the original compiler of the stanzas and stories known as Fă-kheu-King (Dhammapada). It informs us, moreover, that the old term "*pi-u*," *i.e.*, Avadânas, was the same as "the Dawn," and that these Avadânas composed the sixth of the twelve sections (aṅgas) that made up the whole

[1] In the Encyclopædia known as Chi-yuen-fă-pao-kha'n-tung-tsung-liu *Catalogue*, Case xci.), this work is also called "Chuh-yau-lun," Kiouen 9, fol. $\frac{26}{1}$. This book deserves attention. It would well repay translation, if the study of Chinese Buddhist books ever commands notice. The verses, I observe, are repeated in each alternate section, as in a "refrain." The Colophon explains that this work belongs to the class known as "In-tou-cho-tsah," *i.e.*, "Indian Miscellanies," perhaps the *Khuddaka-nikâya* of the South.

Buddhist Canon. The author of the Chinese Preface has mistaken Avadâna (pi-u, *i.e.*, *comparison*; although, as Burnouf states, it is difficult to account for this explanation of the word. *Int. Bud.* 64) for Nidâna; for it is the Nidânas that compose the sixth of the twelve parts of the Buddhist Canon (aṅgas), and as the word Nidânam is confessedly used to signify "the narrative of the circumstances under which any sermon of Buddha was delivered" (Childers, Pâli Dict. *sub voce*), it may be very well applied to the narratives or stories which explain the circumstances under which the stanzas composing Dhammapada were first delivered. The title, "The Dawn," or "Coming forth of Light," is a very usual and significant one to indicate the "origin" or "cause," and in this sense is a proper rendering of Nidâna. The preface goes on to state that a Shaman Saṅghbhadanga of Ki-pin (Cabul) came to Tchangan (Siganfu) about the nineteenth year of the period Kien-Yuen.[1] Having travelled back to India and returned with a copy of the present work, it was eventually translated by Fo-nien, with the assistance of others. Without going through this voluminous work, we way observe that the whole of the first volume, comprising seventy-four double pages, is occupied with the subject "Impermanency," in which there are stories *on* stories, and verses *on* verses, most of which appear to be artificially made for one another; the second subject is "Desire," which occupies twenty-one pages; the third is "Lust," which occupies seventeen pages; the fourth section, however, seems to throw some light on the difference occurring between the tenth chapter of the Chinese earlier versions and the second of the Pâli; in the first the subject is "Carelessness," in the second it is "Reflection;" now in the version we are considering the subject is restored to the

[1] So far as I can make out, this must have been about 345 A.D., although in the *Hai-kwo-tu-chi* the period Kien-Yuen only lasted two years.

Pâli form by the addition of a simple adjunct "Wou;" instead of "Fong-min" (carelessness) as in the former copies, we have here "wou-fong-min," *i.e.*, "absence of Carelessness," or "Reflection," as in the Southern copy. This may perhaps show that the original used by Fo-nien was not altogether uncanonical. We may add that the whole number of chapters in this work is thirty-three, and that the last is, like the Pâli, on "the Brâhmāna." There are ample commentaries attached to many of the verses, so that, after all, this work is of considerable value, and deserving of close examination.

With respect to the last version of the Dhammapada in Chinese, I can only say that it is still assigned to Dharmatrâta as its author,[1]—but there is no resemblance in it to the earlier translation. I shall not attempt, therefore, to institute any comparison between it and the Southern copy, agreement with which alone could make any notice of it in the present work interesting or useful.

I have selected the second Chinese version for translation in preference to the first, because of its completeness. If my object had been to institute a comparison between the Pâli and Chinese copies of Dhammapada, the earlier version would doubtless have been the one to select for the purpose. But such is not the aim of the present book. Its purpose is to show the method adopted by the early Buddhist teachers and preachers who were mainly instrumental in diffusing a knowledge of this religion through the Eastern world. The simple method of Parable was the one used. Doubtless it was this method which, in the first place, contributed to the wide prevalence of the system, and has since enabled it to keep its hold on the minds of so many millions of people. And when we consider the peculiar simplicity of these tales, and the truth contained

[1] *Vide* Catalogue of the Chinese Tripiṭaka, Case LXXVII., p. 95. The translation was made so late as the Sung dynasty (800 or 900 A.D.), and is, therefore, very corrupt.

in the morals drawn from them, we do not wonder at the result; nor can it be questioned that the influence of such teaching must have been beneficial to those affected by it.

With regard to the critical uses to be made of the expressions herein contained, it will suffice to add that my own conviction expressed many years since respecting the primitive idea of Nirvâna, that it was designed to denote a state of rest and peace, resulting from the absence of sorrow and the delusions of sense, is in this work completely confirmed; nor can I see anything in Mr. D'Alwis' remarks on the subject to weaken this conviction. However, this contention is in the hands of other champions, well able from their knowledge of the matter and of the Pâli language, to conduct it to a fair issue, and with them I leave it.

My hope is that some of our younger students (especially those already grounded in Sanscrit) may be induced to take up the subject of "Buddhism in China." It is one which has abundant claims on the attention of the student of religion, but especially on the philanthropist and the missionary,[1] and it is my firm belief that comparatively little will be done either in producing an intelligible version of the Christian Scriptures in countries where Buddhism prevails (especially China and Japan), or in placing the doctrines of the Christian religion fairly and clearly before the people of those countries, until Buddhism is studied by every missionary, and its terminology understood, as it ought to be, by those who constantly use the same terms, in a sense more or less diverse and sometimes directly opposite.[2]

The books now in England offer a large and open field

[1] There are some excellent remarks regarding the duties of missionaries in their work amongst Buddhists, in the introduction to M. Wassilief's "Buddhism," by M. Ed. Laboulaye, pp. viii., xvi. Compare also some remarks respecting incorrect translations of religious phrases, by the late Dr. Ballantyne, "Christianity contrasted with Hindu Philosophy," Introduction, pp. viii., ix.

[2] The expression used by the Ro-

for investigation, and the delight which the study of works wholly unknown to the European world must naturally afford, ought to be a sufficient inducement to tempt those who have the leisure to engage in this pursuit, and to prosecute it with determination.

man Catholic missionaries for "God" (tien chu), is the common term in Buddhist books for "Indra," or, as we should say, "Jupiter." Almost every page of the New Testament version used by Protestant missionaries in China, has some expression or other which would convey to the mind of the Buddhist, either a perverted idea, or else one repugnant to his prejudices. Such expressions ought, therefore, to be explained.

FA-KHEU-KING TSU.

(COD. I.)

PREFACE TO THE SÛTRA CALLED FA-KHEU.

(LAW-VERSES. DHAMMAPADA.)

[*From the Chinese.*]

THE verses called Dhammapada (*Tan-poh*) are selections from all the Sûtras. The expression *Tan* means law, and the word *poh* means verse or sentence. These are various editions (or arrangements) of this Dhammapada Sûtra. There is one with 900 verses, another with 700, and another with 500. Now the word for verse, or Gâthâ, signifies an extract from the Scriptures arranged according to metre. These are the words of Buddha himself, spoken as occasion suggested, not at any one time, but at various times, and the cause and end of their being spoken is also related in the different Sûtras. Now Buddha, the All-wise, moved by compassion for the world, was manifested in the world, to instruct men and lead them into the right way. What he said and taught has been included in twelve sorts of works. There are, however, other collections containing the choice portion of his doctrine, such, for instance, as the four works known as the Âgamas. After Buddha left the world, Ânanda collected a certain number of volumes, in each of which the words of Buddha are quoted, whether the Sûtra be large or small, with this introductory phrase, "Thus have I heard." The place where the sermon was preached is also given, and the occasion and circumstances of it. It was from these works that the Shamans, in after years, copied out the various Gâthâs, some of four lines, some of six lines, and attached to each set a title according to the subject therein explained. But all these verses, without exception, are taken from some one or other of the accepted Scriptures, and therefore they are called Law-verses (or Scripture extracts), because they are found in the Canon.

Now the common edition used by people generally is the one with 700 Gâthas. The meaning of these Gâthâs is sometimes very obscure (deep), and men say that there is no meaning at all in them. But let them consider that as it is difficult to meet with a teacher like Buddha, so the words of Buddha are naturally hard of explanation. Moreover, all the literature of this religion is written in the language of India, which widely differs from that of China—the language and the books, in fact, are those of the Devas (Heaven). So to translate them faithfully is not an easy task.

The present work, the original of which consisted of 500 verses, was brought from India in the third year of the reign of Hwang-wu (A.D. 223), by Wai-chi-lan, and, with the help of another Indian called Tsiang-im, was first explained, and then translated into Chinese. On some objection being made as to the inelegance of the phrases employed, Wai-chi-lan stated "that the words of Buddha are holy words, not merely elegant or tasteful, and that his Law is not designed to attract persons by its pleasing character, but by its deep and spiritual meaning."

Finally, the work of translation was finished, and afterwards 13 additional sections added, making up the whole to 752 verses, 14,580 words, and headings of chapters, 39.

DHAMMAPADA,

OR

VERSES FROM THE LAW,

WITH ACCOMPANYING PARABLES.

A SÛTRA (COD. 2.)

TRANSLATED BY THE SHAMANS FĂ-KHEU AND FA-LIH, OF THE WESTERN TSIN DYNASTY.

SECTION I.

IMPERMANENCY (ANICCATÂ).

1. THE first parable[1] in this section relates that Śakra having on one occasion been conceived in the household of a potter, as the offspring of the female ass that turned the mill, the ass, overjoyed at the prospect of progeny, kicked her heels up, and broke all the pitchers and pots which the master had made. On this the man, taking a stick, belaboured the beast to such a degree, that the newly-formed fœtus was destroyed, and the prospect of

[1] This parable is the same in Cod. i. and ii. It differs in Cod. iii. In the last name, the scene of the story is at Vaisâlî. The sermon was designed to show the comparative worthlessness of all earthly grandeur. The argument was derived from the gaudy equipages of the youths of Vaisâlî, who drove to the Vihâra where Buddha was (the Monkey-tank Vihâra) in their variously-adorned chariots. [But in Cod. iii. the verse occurs after the *third* story.]

offspring cut off. On which occasion Buddha repeated these lines—

"Whatever exists[1] (*sanskâra*) is without endurance. And hence the terms "flourishing" and "decaying."[2] A man is born, and then he dies. Oh, the happiness of escaping from this condition! For the life of men is but as the earthen vessels made in a potter's mill; formed with such care, they are all destined to destruction."

Śakra, having heard these verses, was enabled to enter on the first path of the Buddhist profession, and obtained peace.

2. On a certain occasion Buddha was residing in the country of Śrâvastî (Sewet). The Râja Prasenajit had been celebrating the funeral obsequies of the queen-mother, aged more than ninety years. On his return, he came to the place where Buddha was and saluted him. On this the great teacher spake thus (after inquiring respecting the occasion of the visit): "There are four things, O Râja! which from the first till now have been the causes of constant anxiety and fear to men—the fear of old age, of disease, of death, and of grief consequent on death. Alas! the life of man is but as the perishing things we see around us; to-day they flourish, to-morrow they are gone. Just as the waters of the five rivers[3] are ever flowing on without cessation day and night, such is the case with man—his life is ever ebbing away." And then the Honoured of the world spoke these words and said—

"As the waters of a river ever hasten on and flow away, and once gone, never return, such is

[1] Ch. *hing*.

[2] The Chinese *fă*, as is well known, has often the meaning I have given it in the text.

[3] Of the *Panjab*?

the life of man. That which is gone knows not any return."

Buddha having further expounded this subject, the King and his attendants dismissed their grief, and, filled with joy, entered the "Paths."[1]

3. On a certain occasion, when Buddha was dwelling in the Bamboo Garden near Râjagriha, he had been preaching in the city, and was returning homewards with his followers when he met a man driving a herd of fat and sleek cattle towards the gates of the town. On this the Honoured of the world took up the subject, and spake as follows:—

"As a man with his staff in his hand[2] goes along tending and pasturing the cattle, so are old age and death, they also watch over the life that perishes; and of all they watch over, there is not one, of whatever class, man or woman, rich or poor, but in the end shall decay and disappear. Every day and night takes from the little space given to each one born; there is the gradual decay of a few years and all is gone, as the waters of a pool are cut off (or exhausted)."

Buddha having arrived at the grove, and having washed his feet and arranged his robes, sat down; on this occasion Ânanda respectfully asked him to explain the verses he had just repeated, on which the Honoured of the world related that the master of the oxen he had just seen sent them forth day by day to pasture and feed, in order that when fattened and well conditioned they might be killed

[1] The "paths" are the four stages in the progress towards complete emancipation. (Compare Max Müller, *Dhammapada*, cix., n.)

[2] This verse seems to agree with No. 135 of the Pâli. (*Catena*, p. 27.)

one by one. "Such," he added, "is the fate of all that lives; it is thus it flourishes for a moment and then dies." On this upwards of two hundred of the hearers obtained spiritual powers,[1] and became Rahats."

4. On one occasion when Buddha was residing at Śrâvastî, in the Garden of Anâthapindada,[2] a certain Brahmachârin,[3] who had lost an only daughter, about fourteen or fifteen years of age, very beautiful and much beloved, being nearly deprived of reason through grief, having heard tidings of the wisdom of the holy one (Buddha), came to him where he was, and laid bare the cause of his unhappiness, on which the teacher took up his discourse, and said—

"There are four things in the world, O Brahmachârin! which cannot permanently last, and what are the four? Thinking we have obtained something that will last, it must needs be we find that it will not continue. Being rich, it must needs be poverty will come. Being united and agreed, there will be division and separation. Being strong and hale, yet there will come death." And then the Honoured of the world added these lines— "That which appears permanent will perish; that which is high will be brought low; where there is agreement, there will come division; and where there is birth, there will be death."

[1] Miraculous power, or, the power to work miracles.

[2] As is well known this person bought for Buddha a site near Śrâvastî, on which the celebrated Jetavana Vihâra was built. There are full accounts in the Chinese Canon of his history, which agree with those found in the south. (Compare the Chinese copy of *Mahâvastu*, K. 6.)

[3] The word "Brahmachârin" occurring throughout this work corresponds to the "Brâhmana" of the Southern version.

On this the Brahmachârin received enlightenment, and having assumed the robes and tonsure of a Bhikshu, he quickly became a Rahat.

5. Once when Buddha was residing in the Gridhrakûta Mountain, near Râjagriha, there was a certain famous courtezan in the city, called "Lien-hwa" (Pundarî, or Padma) most beautiful in form, and incomparable for grace. This woman, wearied of her mode of life, resolved to join herself to Buddha and become a Bhikshuni. Accordingly she proceeded towards the place where he was, and having half ascended the mountain, she halted awhile at a fountain of water to drink; whilst lifting the water to her mouth she saw her face reflected in the fountain, and she could not but observe her own incomparable beauty, the delicacy of her complexion, her rosy hair, her graceful figure. On seeing herself thus she altered her mind, and said—"Shall one born so beautiful as I am go out of the world and become a recluse?—no! rather let me have my fill of pleasure and be satisfied"—on this she made ready to turn back and go home. But in the meantime Buddha, seeing the circumstance, and knowing that Pundarî was in a condition to be saved (converted), transformed himself at once into a beautiful woman, infinitely more charming than Pundarî. Meeting as they went, the courtezan was amazed at the beauty of the strange woman, and asked her, "Whence come you, fair one? and where dwell your kindred? and why do you travel thus alone without attendants?" On which the stranger replied, "I am returning to yonder city, and though we be not acquainted, let us join company and go together." On this they went on their way till they came to a certain fountain on the road, where they sat down. At length, the conversation having ceased, the strange beauty, resting herself against the knees of Pundarî, fell asleep. After a time the courtezan, looking down on her friend, was amazed to behold her form entirely changed;

she had become loathsome as a corpse, her face pallid, her teeth gone, the hair fallen from her head, hateful insects feeding on her flesh. Frightened and aghast at the sight, Pundarî hastened away from the spot, and as she exclaimed "How transient is human beauty!" she hurried back again in the direction of Buddha's dwelling-place, and having arrived, cast herself prostrate at his feet, and related to him what she had seen, on which Buddha addressed her thus—"There are four things, Pundarî, which must ever cause sadness and disappointment. That one, however beautiful, must yet become old; that one, however firmly established, must die; that one bound in closest ties of relationship and affection, must yet be separated from those he loves; and that wealth, heaped up in ever such profusion, must yet be scattered and lost." And then the World-honoured added these lines, and said—

"Old age brings with it loss of all bodily attraction; through decay and disease a man perishes; his body bent, and his flesh withered, this is the end of life. What use is this body when it lies rotting beside the flowings of the Ganges? It is but the prison-house of disease, and of the pains of old age and death. To delight in pleasure, and to be greedy after self-indulgence, is but to increase the load of sin, forgetting the great change that must come, and the inconstancy of human life. With no son to depend upon, without father or brother; Death pressing at the door—without a friend (relation) to look to for aid."

The courtezan having heard these words, was able to see that life is but as the flower, that there is nought permanent but Nirvâna, and so she requested permission to become a Bhikshunî, which being readily granted, she assumed the robes and the tonsure, and soon became a Rahat, and all the rest who heard the words of Buddha were filled with inexpressible joy.

6. In days of old when Buddha was dwelling in the Bamboo Garden near Râjagriha, preaching the Law, there was a certain Brahmachârin and his three brothers, who had obtained spiritual perception, and thereby knew that after seven days they would have to die. On which they said—"By our spiritual power we can overturn heaven and earth, touch the sun and moon, move mountains, and check the flowing torrent, but yet after all we cannot arrest death." Then one said, "I will seek out in the depths of ocean this Demon of inconstancy and destroy him." Another said, "I will rend Mount Sumeru in twain, and enter there to seek this Demon of inconstancy to destroy him." Another said, "I will mount into remotest space to seek the Demon of inconstancy and destroy him." Another said, "I will enter the bowels of the earth to seek him and destroy him." The King of the country having heard of these men, came to Buddha to inquire respecting the point, on which the Honoured of the world explained that there were four things which, whilst we are in the world (*yin*), cannot be escaped. 1st, It is impossible to avoid birth in some form or other; 2d, Having been born it is impossible to escape old age; 3d, When old, it is impossible to escape infirmity and disease; 4th, Under these circumstances, it is impossible to escape death—and then he added these verses and said—

"Neither in space, nor in the depths of ocean,[1]

[1] This verse agrees with v. 128 of the Southern version. It occurs in Cod. iii. K. II. fol. $\frac{6}{1}$. I would here notice (by the way) how singularly curt and definite these verses of Dhammapada are; take, *e.g.*, the *pada* preceding the one just named in Cod. iii. "Doing evil, you will go to Hell. Doing good (or "preparing," or "practising" good), you will

nor in the hidden fastness of the mountain, nor in any other place can death be escaped. It is by knowing this and reflecting upon it that the Bhikshu is able to overthrow the army of Mâra and obtain deliverance from birth and death."[1]

go to Heaven. If you are able to *persevere* in the good path, then without any remnants (of sorrow) you will enter Nirvâna."

[1] In Cod. iii. we have numerous verses under the heading of this chapter, among which I observe on fol. 9 and 10 the stanza, numbered 146 in the Southern copy.

"What joy? What laughter? let us recollect the everlasting burnings! Lost in deepest gloom, why seek ye not the Light?" [The "everlasting burnings" are explained in the Commentary as those resulting from sorrow and pain.] As a further instance of epigram in these verses, I would refer to Cod. iii. K. II. Ψ^{5}. "The Sun which shines to-day once set, so much less of life remains! Ah! what joy can there be in this condition, resembling the fish in ever-shallowing waters." [With respect to "burning," as the result of sin—consult v. 136, n. Max Müller, Dh.]

SECTION II.

INCITING TO WISDOM.[1]

1. THIS section consisting of twenty-nine verses,[2] is designed to excite listless mendicants to renewed exertion in the path of Duty. The first four gâthas were spoken by Buddha in the Jetavana at Śrâvastî. On this occasion a careless disciple had left the company of his hearers, whilst he was preaching on the necessity of *exertion* in casting off the hindrances and trammels that prevent advance in a religious life. Having retired to the interior of his cell, he indulged himself in sleep and effeminacy —not knowing that after seven days he would die. Whereupon Buddha addressed him thus:

"Alas! arise thou![3] why sleeping there? a companion of the spider, and the creeping insect. Hidden from sight, practising impurity, miserably deceived with regard to the character of the body (or Life), even as one who dreads the amputation of a diseased limb, his heart heavy, and his affliction great, seeks forgetfulness in sleep, but nevertheless cannot escape the recollection of his coming calamity—such is your case. But the man who strives after true wisdom,[4] feels no such sorrow, always reflecting on religion, he forgets himself—

[1] Chinese "kian hioh." We observe that in Cod. iii. the title of this second chapter is "Desire" or "Lust" (Tanhâ), and its verses agree with 212, ss. of the Pâli.

[2] That is in Cod. ii.

[3] There is some similarity here with § 168 and the Southern copy.

[4] Literally "understands the character (outline) of virtue."

possessed of right apprehension of Truth he increases in wisdom daily, he becomes a light in the world; however born,[1] his happiness is a thousand fold greater, and in the end he shall escape every evil mode of existence."

Hearing these verses the mendicant arose and came before Buddha, and prostrated himself in his presence; on which the World-honoured asked him if he knew his former states of existence; the mendicant confessed that owing to the indulgence of his carnal desires, he was unable to penetrate such mysteries—on which the teacher explained how in the time of a former Buddha he had been a disciple, but had given way to self-indulgence and sleep—on account of which he had been born for many thousand years, as an insect, and in other similar forms—but now his evil Karma exhausted, he had again been born as a man and become a mendicant. On hearing this the Shaman, struck with remorse, repented of his sin and became a Rahat.

2. Formerly, when Buddha was residing at Śrâvastî, in the Jetavana, whilst preaching for the benefit of the four orders of his followers, there was a young Bhikshu, who being overcome by foolish thoughts, was unable to restrain his desires. Grieved at this, he resolved to dismember himself, and for that purpose he went to the house of his Patron (dânapati), and having procured a knife he proceeded to his cell, and sitting on his couch he began to reflect on the evil which resulted from the power of gratifying desire. Buddha knowing his thoughts, and perceiving him to be deceived by ignorance of the true cause of his conduct, an ill-restrained mind, proceeded to his cell, and inquired what he was going to do. On this the Bhikshu explained that as he was unable to check

[1] Or, "whatever is born, its happiness is a thousandfold greater," *i.e.*, in consequence of *his* virtue.

desire, and in consequence to advance in religious exercise, he was about to dismember himself. On this Buddha explained that uncertainty and doubt were the causes of delay in religious progress, that the first thing to do was to govern the mind, and restrain the thoughts, without which merely to get rid of the external instrument of evil was useless, and then he added these lines—

"Learning first to cut off the Mother, and to follow the one true guide (Minister), dismissing all the subordinate place-holders, this is (the conduct of) the truly enlightened man."

And then explaining that "Doubt" was the Mother, and the twelve causes and effects"[1] the subordinates, whilst Wisdom was the one Minister, the Bhikshu obtained enlightenment, and was at rest.

3. Formerly, when Buddha was residing in the Gridhrakûta Mountain near Râjagriha preaching the Law of Eternal Life (*i.e.*, Nirvâna) to the assembled multitudes, there was a certain obdurate and hardened Bhikshu present, on whom the words of the Preacher had no effect. On this Buddha, knowing his thoughts, sent him to the back of the mountains to meditate beneath a tree in the middle of the gorge, known as that of the "Evil Spirits"—with a view to his casting away the impediments that prevented him from attaining Nirvâna. Arrived at the spot he was constantly alarmed and interrupted by the sounds of the evil spirits, though he saw no form, and so instead of arriving at a fixed state of composure, he rather desired to go back to the place whence he came—but on reflecting that the sounds he heard were only those of evil spirits who wished to drive him from his purpose, he stayed where he was. Then Buddha coming near him as he sat, took his place beside him and said—"Have you no fear dwelling alone in this solitary place?" to which he replied—"At

[1] The Nidânas.

first when I had scarcely yet entered on this part of the Mountain, I was for a moment filled with fear—but then a wild elephant coming to the place were I was, and lying down close to me under a Tree, went to sleep, as though he were perfectly rejoiced to get away from the rest of the herd, and be at peace (and so I was re-assured)." Then Buddha, knowing perfectly the circumstances of the case, said, "That elephant was but one of a herd of five hundred, who from fear that he might be captured with the rest, found his joy in separation, and a solitary life—how much more, then, should you seek for happiness in leaving your home, and practising in solitude the rules of an ascetic life?" and then he added these verses—

"Perceiving that the ignorant herd can never attain true Wisdom,[1] the wise man prefers in solitude to guard himself in virtuous conduct, not associating with the foolish; rejoicing in the practice of moral duties (*sila*), and pursuing such conduct as becomes this mode of life, there is no need of a companion or associate in such practice—solitary in virtue, without sorrow, a man rejoices as the wild elephant (escaped from the herd)."

On hearing these words the Bhikshu obtained rest, and the "Evil Spirits" also, who listened and understood them, were so awed that they vowed never again to molest solitary ascetics, and then Buddha and the mendicant returned to their place.

4. On a certain occasion when Buddha was residing in the Jetavana at Śrâvastî, preaching for the good of Devas and men, two new disciples from Râjagriha desired to go to the place where he was to see him. Between the two countries there was an uninhabited and inhospitable desert. Parched with the heat and utterly exhausted, they came

[1] The expression "Shen yau" is used in a Buddhist sense for "Bôdhi."

at length to a pool of water and sat down, eagerly desiring to slake their thirst. But they perceived that the water was full of insects, and so hesitated to drink. At length one said, "If I drink not I shall not be able to see Buddha, the end justifies the means," and so he drank of the water. The other, considering that the Law of Buddha was one of universal love, which forbade the taking of life, refused to drink, and as the other went on his way alone, the latter died and was born in Heaven. Then considering the circumstances of his former life, he quickly descended and came to the place where Buddha was and saluted him. In a short time the first also arrived at the place, and on Buddha asking him whence he came and where his companion was, he related with tears all the circumstances of the case, on which the Teacher, pointing to the bright Deva come down from Heaven, assured the other that this was his former companion; he had kept the Law and was born in Heaven, and was the first to behold the form of Buddha; but you "who say you see me, and yet have transgressed my Law, are not seen by me, but are as though you were distant ten thousand li, whereas this man who has kept the Law, dwells ever in my sight," and the World-honoured one added these lines, and said—

"The obedient disciple who follows the precepts without fail, in either world (Heaven or earth) exalted, he shall obtain his desire and aim (his prayer). But, on the other hand, the disciple who is stint in obedience, not keeping the precepts in their strictness, in either world grievously afflicted, mourns for his former vows (unaccomplished). Yet both,[1] if they persevere in their inquiries and search, shall be saved from error, although with difficulty."

On hearing these words the disciple who had erred was overjoyed, and arrived at enlightenment.

[1] It is possible the expression may refer to the *second* only.

SECTION III.

THE DISCIPLE, OR "ŚRÂVAKA."

1. ONCE on a time in Śrâvastî there was a certain housewife, poor though she was, who had no religious principle, and was without faith. Buddha seeing her condition was moved with pity. He saw that, whenever his followers went begging through the city, they met with nothing but abuse at the door of this woman's house. On a Shaman expostulating with her, on the ground that he only sought alms as a religious duty, she said, "If you were dying I would give you nothing, much less now that you are hale and well." On this the Shaman, standing before her, assumed the condition of one who was really dead. The various functions of his body ceased, and from his mouth and nose crept in and out the hateful insects that accompany death. On seeing this ghastly sight, the woman fell down in a swoon, and so remained. Meanwhile the Shaman, by his spiritual power, transported himself thence a few *lis*, and, sitting beneath a tree, composed himself to contemplation. Meantime the husband of the woman returning, and finding his wife in the condition related, inquired the reason of it, on which she replied that she had been frightened by a rascally Shaman. On this the husband in a rage seized his bow and his sword, and set out to pursue and avenge himself on the mendicant. Coming to where he was, the Shaman, by his spiritual power, surrounded himself with a wall, through which there were gates of approach, but all were closed. The incensed husband, being unable to get at the mendicant, asked him to open the gates; on which he replied, "Lay aside your bow and your sword and you

may enter." On this the man thought, "Even if I leave my weapons behind me I shall be able to maul him with my fists." On this he put down his bow and sword, and asked again for admission. But the Shaman said, "The gate cannot be opened, for the bow and the sword which you must lay aside are not those weapons you carried in your hand, but the enmity and malice that fill your heart; lay these aside and you may enter." On this the man, struck with the conviction of his sin, both he and his wife repented of their evil designs and became disciples—on which occasion the enlightened follower of Buddha (man of Bôdhi, or religious man) added these words, and said—

"The disciple (Śrâvaka) who is able to hold (the precepts) firmly, like a wall, difficult to be overturned, surrounds himself with the protection of the Law, and thus persevering perfects himself in saving wisdom. The disciple, with his mind enlightened, by this enlightenment adds yet to his store of wisdom, and so obtains perfect insight into the mysteries of Religion (Truth), and thus illumined, he practises the duties of his calling in peace. The disciple, able to cast away (the causes of) sorrow, in perfect rest enjoys happiness, and by virtuously preaching the Law of Eternal Life, himself obtains Nirvâna. By hearing, he acquaints himself with the Rules of a Holy Life; he shakes off doubt and becomes settled in faith. By hearing, he is able to resist all that is contrary to the Law (Truth, or Religion), and so advancing, he arrives at the place where there is no more Death."

On hearing these words the man and his wife, beholding the wonderful signs of Buddha displayed in the person of this disciple, smote on their breasts in penitence, and countless thousands, like themselves, throughout the world, were converted and saved.

2. In old time, when Buddha was residing in the country of Kausâmbî, in a certain Vihâra called Mei-yin (beautiful voice), and preaching for the sake of the four orders, there was a certain Brahmachârin, unrivalled for knowledge of Scripture, who being unable to find any one equal to himself in argument, was accustomed to carry, wherever he went, a lighted Torch in his hand. One day a man in the market-place of a certain town, seeing him thus, asked him the reason of his strange conduct, on which he replied —"The world is so dark, and men so deluded, that I carry this Torch to light it up so far as I can."[1] At this time Buddha transformed himself into a man of eminence (magistrate), who, sitting on his chair of office in the market-place, forthwith called out to the Brahmachârin, "What ho there! what are you about (with that Torch)?" To whom the Brahmachârin replied, "All men are so wrapped in ignorance and gloom, that I carry this Torch to illumine them." Then the magistrate asked him again, "And are you so learned as to be acquainted with the four treatises (vidyâs) which occur in the midst of the Sacred Books, to wit, the treatise on Literature (Śabdavidyâ); the treatise on the "Heavenly Bodies and their Paths;" the treatise on "Government;" and the treatise on "Military Art"? On the Brahmachârin being forced to confess he was unacquainted with these things, he flung away his Torch, and Buddha appearing in his glorious body, added these words—

"If any man, whether he be learned or not, consider himself so great as to despise other men, he is like a blind man holding a candle—blind himself, he illumines others."

On hearing these words the Brahmachârin sought to become a disciple of Buddha, and was accordingly admitted.

[1] This recalls the story of Diogenes and his lantern.

3. There was in former days a certain nobleman, called Su-ta (Sudatta ?), residing at Śrâvastî, who had become a disciple of Buddha, and entered on the first path. He had a friend called "Hau-shi" (Sudana ?), who was not a believer. On this latter falling sick, and finding no help in any one for whose advice he sent, his friend Sudatta resolved to send for Buddha, and ask him to visit his friend. In compliance with the request Buddha came, and, with his body glorious as the sun, entered the house of Sudana, and sat down. [He then preached a sermon on the moral diseases to which men are liable, and afterwards added these lines]:

"The office of the Sun is to give light; the office of a Father, to be kind and compassionate; the office of a Ruler is to restrain and govern; the office of a Man of Reason (religious man) is to listen to instruction; a physician concerns himself with prolonging the life of men; a warrior desires victory; and so Religion (the Law) resides in the possession of wisdom. A happy walk through life is the gladness of the world; a friend is for consultation; the choice of a companion is for the occasion which requires him; to behold the beauty of women is the joy of the chamber; the proof of wisdom is in speaking; to be a Ruler one must be able to discriminate rightly; to dispel doubt and error, one must exercise the light of supreme wisdom (Bôdhi); to search out the foundation of rest and quiet, one must be able faithfully to hold (observe) the Treasures of the Law (the Scriptures). He who hears is able to be of advantage to the present world, his wife, children, and friends, and in the next world to arrive at perfect happiness. Still hearing, he arrives at the perfection of sacred knowledge, and is able to discriminate and explain the secrets of Truth; and thus he governs himself without transgression; receiving the Law, he extols that which is right, and so obtains release from all (moral) disease, he dissipates all the causes of sorrow and pain, he excludes all possibility of misfortune or calamity, he is always successful in finding a ground for peace and comfort: such are the consequences following in the life of one who 'hears much' (the Śrâvaka)."

On hearing this sermon, the sick man was convinced of the Truth and became a disciple.

4. In times gone by, there was to the south of Râjagriha a great mountain, distant from the city about 200 li. Through this mountain there was a pass deep and lonely, through which the road to South India lay. Five hundred robbers had taken up their abode in this defile, who used to murder and spoil all travellers that passed that way. The king had vainly sent to capture them, but they always escaped. Buddha, residing in the neighbourhood, and considering the case of these men, that they understood not the nature of their conduct, and that although he had come into the world to teach men, yet their eyes had not seen him, nor their ears heard the tidings of his Law, he resolved to go to them. Consequently he transformed himself into a man richly dight, on a well-caparisoned steed, with his sword and bow, with bags of silver and gold on his saddle-bow, and precious stones studding his horse's bravery.

On entering the defile loud neighed his steed. On hearing the sound the 500 robbers started up, and spying the traveller, exclaimed, "Never have we had such prospect of booty; let us up, and capture him!" So they proceeded to surround the traveller, with a view to prevent his escape;

but he, with one shot of his bow, pierced the 500, and with one stroke of his sword wounded them.

On their falling to the ground, they exclaimed, "What God is this? Oh that he would draw out these arrows, and assuage the bitter pain of such wounds as ours!" On this the traveller began to explain that such hurts as these were trivial compared with the pain caused by the sorrow that rules the world, and the wounds of unbelief and doubt, and that nought but the wisdom resulting from earnest attention (hearing) to the Scriptures could heal such wounds; and then he added these words and said:

"There is no painful wound so bad as sorrow—no piercing arrow so sharp as folly. Nothing can remedy these but an earnest attention to religious instruction. From this the blind receive sight, the deluded are enlightened. Men are guided and led by this, as eyes given to him without eyes. This, then, is able to dispel unbelief, to remove sorrow, to impart joy; the highest wisdom is the lot of those who 'hear.' This is the title of him who has acquired the greatest merit (most to be revered)."

On hearing this the robbers repented of their evil lives, and the arrows, of themselves, left their bodies, and their wounds were healed. They then became disciples, and obtained rest and peace.

SECTION IV.

SIMPLE FAITH.

1. In the days of old, to the south-east of Śrâvastî, there was a great River, very deep and wide, on the banks of which there was a hamlet, consisting of some 500 houses, the inhabitants of which had not yet heard the news of Salvation, and were consequently immersed entirely in worldliness and selfish pursuits.

The Honoured of the world, ever thinking on the salvation of men, resolved to go to this village and preach to the people. Accordingly, he came to the river-side, and sat down beneath a tree. The village people, seeing the glory of his appearance, approached with reverence to worship him. After they had so done, Buddha began to preach to them, but they believed him not. On this Buddha caused the appearance of a man coming from the south side of the river, where the water was very deep and the current strong, walking on the surface of it; and so coming, he approached Buddha, and, bowing down, worshipped him.

All the people, seeing this appearance, asked the man in astonishment, whence he had come, "for we never in all our lives have seen such a sight as this, a man walking on the surface of the water. Tell us, then, by what artifice has this been done, and how it was you were not engulphed in the stream." On which the man replied: "I reside on the southern bank of the river, and had ever lived in ignorance and folly till I heard that Buddha was here teaching the way of deliverance, on which, coming to the bank of the river, and not having time to wait to be carried over, I asked the men if it was deep, and whether I could not cross over without a boat. On which they said, 'Oh yes! you can cross without fear.' On this I walked over, because I believed. Simply this and nothing more enabled me to do so." On this Buddha said: "It is well spoken—well spoken. Faith like yours alone can save the world from the yawning gulf of continual birth and death; such faith alone can enable them to walk across dryshod (to the other shore)," and then he added these lines:

"Faith can cross the flood, even as the master of the ship (steers his bark across the sea); ever advancing in the conquest of sorrow, wisdom lands us on yonder shore. The wise man who lives by faith, in virtue of his holy life, enjoys unselfish[1] bliss, and casts off all shackles. Faith lays hold of true wisdom (or finds the path); Religion leads to deliverance from death; from hearing comes knowledge, which brings with it enlightenment; faith, with obedience (moral conduct), is the path of wisdom: firmly persevering in this, a man finds escape from pain, and is thus able to pass over and escape the gulf of destruction."

Hearing these words, these villagers were filled with joy, and embracing the five rules, were enabled to believe on Buddha.

2. When Buddha was living in the world there was a certain nobleman called Su-lo-to (Śraddha?), of great wealth, who from a principle of faith had resolved to entertain Buddha and his disciples on the eighth day of every month in Lent (*i.e.*, the months of rain); but on these occasions none of his sons or grandsons ever made their appearance, being engrossed in other matters. At

[1] Wou-wei.

length the nobleman died, and as none of the children cared about entertaining Buddha, a servant boy called Pi-lo-to (Vraddah?) resolved to do so. Consequently, having borrowed 500 pieces of money, he proceeded to invite the Master and his 1200 disciples to his house. After the entertainment and the departure of the guests, he went to rest; when lo! on waking the next morning, he found his house full of silver and gold and all precious substances.

On going to Buddha, the Master explained that this was the result of his faith, and then added these lines:

"Faith is wealth! Obedience is wealth! Modesty also is wealth! Hearing is wealth, and so is Charity! Wisdom is sevenfold riches. Walking by Faith,[1] ever pure, a man perceives the Truth (the Law). Wisdom is as sandals on the feet to him who walks. To receive with respect instruction, and not forget it, this, whoever he be, and however born, is wealth: no question is asked whether he be male or female, it is this alone that will bring gain at the last. Whosoever is wise will understand these truths."

Having heard these words, Pi-lo-to was enabled to believe, and became a disciple; and so his wife also, and his children.

[1] Literally "From a motive of Faith guarding (or keeping) the Precepts."

SECTION V.

CAREFUL OBSERVANCE OF MORAL DUTIES.

I. ABOUT forty or fifty li to the south of Benares there was formerly a mountain in which five Shamans dwelt, practising religious discipline. Every morning they used to leave their abode and go a-begging for their food, and then return to the mountain, sometimes, however, not till late in the evening, after which they gave themselves up to strict meditation. And yet, though years had passed by, they had not attained to Reason (Bôdhi). Buddha, pitying their condition, transformed himself into a religious man, and going to their abode, asked them, saying, Have you attained the object of your religious exercises or not? And then the ascetics explained that, although they had strictly adhered to the rules of their profession, and daily practised self-denial and meditation, yet they had failed to arrive at the end, *i.e.*, true peace and rest. On this, the stranger desired them to remain in their abode on the morrow, and let him bring them their food, and so rest themselves awhile; and so for several successive days he supplied their wants, whilst they were on their part filled with satisfaction, and enabled to rise above the mere formal attention to duty; and then the stranger added these lines, and said:

"The Bhikshu, who adheres to the strict rules of a religious life, who guards and controls all his senses, takes his food in moderation, sleeps according to necessity, by these rules subduing his mind, keeping his thoughts in close subjection,[1] inwardly enlightened by wisdom and meditation, never forsaking the right path (path of Bôdhi): thus inwardly illumined, observing the rules of right conduct, satisfied as to the character of true wisdom, proceeding onward in the path of daily duty, this man, at rest in himself, shall get rid of all sorrow."

The stranger having thus spoken, lo! the glorious body of Buddha shone forth, and the five men were converted, and obtained the condition of Rahats.

[1] Chi-kwan.

SECTION VI.

ON REFLECTION.

1. In olden time, when Buddha was in the world, a certain Râja called Fo-kia-sha[1] was a friend of Bimbisâra Râja; the first, however, was not a believer in Buddha, as Bimbisâra was. On a certain occasion Vaksha had sent seven precious umbrellas (chattas) to his friend Bimbisâra. On receiving them, the latter offered them to Buddha, and said, "My friend, Vaksha Râja, has presented me with these precious umbrellas! Pray permit me to offer them to you, with the intention that his heart may be convinced and his eyes opened to behold Buddha, and he be thus led to receive your doctrine, and reverence the Holy Assembly as his reward." Then Buddha replied: "Bimbasâra Râja, cause to be written the Sûtra of the twelve Nidânas, and present the book to that king in return for the seven precious umbrellas; and his heart will be enlightened (or, receive deliverance wrought by Faith)." [Accordingly Bimbisâra did so, and his friend, in consequence, was convinced and became a disciple; and finally gave up the kingdom to his son. Having failed to obtain an interview with Buddha, although he had frequently met him in begging through the streets of Râjagriha, the Teacher at length caused the appearance of a Shaman to meet the king, and explain to him that by reflection on the work in his possession he might truly behold Buddha; and to this he added these words]:—

"The man who takes refuge in Buddha, this is

[1] (Vaksha?).

the man who obtains real advantage. Night and day, therefore, he ought ever to reflect on Buddha, the Law and the Church. Being thus truly enlightened, this man is a disciple of Buddha. Thus reflecting continually on the three Treasures, and on impermanency, and his own body,[1] reflecting on moral duty, on charity, on the emptiness of all things around him, and their unreality (without marks), these are subjects for consideration."

[On hearing these words Vaksha entered on the third path, and obtained rest.]

[1] Or, on himself.

SECTION VII.

ON LOVE OR MERCIFULNESS [*Mettâ*].

1. IN old times, Buddha was residing in a country about 500 li from Râjagriha, full of mountains. In these mountains there lived a certain clan of about 122 persons, who occupied themselves in hunting, and fed themselves on the flesh of the animals they killed. [Buddha goes to the place and converts the women, who were left alone during the day, whilst their husbands were hunting, and then adds these lines]:

"He who is humane does not kill (or, it is humane not to kill); he is ever able to preserve (his own?) life. This principle (*chu*) is imperishable; whoever observes it, no calamity shall betide that man. Politeness, indifference to worldly things, hurting no one, without place for annoyance—this is the character of the Brahma Heaven (or of Brahma Deva). Ever exercising love towards the infirm; pure, according to the teaching of Buddha; knowing when sufficient has been had; knowing when to stop,—this is to escape (the recurrence of) Birth and Death."[1]

[The women, having heard these words, were converted, and on the men's return, although they wished at first to kill Buddha, they were restrained by their wives; and,

[1] These Gâthâs are very obscure.

listening to his words of love, they also were converted]. And then he added these lines:

"There are eleven advantages which attend the man who practises mercifulness, and is tender to all that lives; his body is always in health (happy); he is blessed with peaceful sleep, and when engaged in study he is also composed; he has no evil dreams, he is protected by Heaven (Devas), and loved by men; he is unmolested by poisonous things, and escapes the violence of war; he is unharmed by fire or water; he is successful wherever he lives, and when dead goes to the heaven of Brahma. These are the eleven."

Having uttered these words, both men and women were admitted into the company of his disciples, and obtained rest.

2. There was, in times gone by, a certain mighty king, called Ho-meh (*love-darkness*), who ruled in a certain district where no tidings of Buddha or his merciful doctrine had yet been heard; but the religious practices were the usual ones of sacrifice and prayer to the gods for protection. Now it happened that the king's mother being sick, the physicians having vainly tried their medicines, all the wise men were called to consult as to the best means of restoring her to health. After several years, during which she did not improve, the Queen mother sent for 200 celebrated Brahmans, and desired them to exercise their supernatural arts in discovering from the sun, moon, and stars a way of recovery. These Brahmans replied: "It is useless so to do, as the heavenly signs are in opposition and not favourable." On the King asking them what should be done, they replied, "Outside the city there should be selected a convenient place, level and plane,

and without pollution, and sacrifices of a hundred beasts of different kinds should be offered on the four hills (or to the four quarters), the sun, moon, and stars, with a young child as a crowning oblation to Heaven. Then the King in his own person, with his mother, going to this place to participate in the sacrifice, the stars and heavenly bodies may be propitiated.[1] [On this Buddha, moved with compassion, came to the spot, and preached a sermon on "Love to all that lives," and added these words]:

"If a man lives a hundred years, and engages the whole of his time and attention in religious offerings to the gods, sacrificing elephants and horses, and other things, all this is not equal to one act of pure love in saving life."

[In consequence of this sermon and the exhibition of the glorious body of Buddha, they were converted, and became disciples.]

[1] Here follows a description of the King ordering a hundred head of elephants, horses, oxen, sheep, to be driven along the road from the Eastern Gate towards the place of sacrifice, and how their piteous cries rang through (shook) heaven and earth.

SECTION VIII.

ON WORDS (CONVERSATION).

I. In former days, when Fo-kia-sha[1] (Vaksha ?) râja was entering the city of Râjagriha to beg his food from door to door, in the city gate there was a cow, just delivered of its calf, which had turned round and gored its master to death. The cow having been sold to a passer-by, he put a rope round its horns, and desired to lead it onwards; but the cow, making an attack in the rear, killed this man also; then the son, in a rage, killed the animal, and cutting it up, exposed it for sale in the market-place. Now a certain person passing by, bought the head of the creature, and carrying it away with him, as he sat down to rest, fastened it on the bough of the tree 'neath which he reposed; all at once, the rope giving way, the head fell down, and the horn, piercing the skull of the man underneath, killed him also. Bimbisâra Râja, hearing of this strange occurrence, how that a cow killed three men in one day, came to Buddha to inquire of him the antecedent causes of this event, on which Buddha related the following history:—
"In former days there were three merchants who, coming to a certain city to transact business, took up their abode in the house of a friendless old woman, and there lodged. Being dissatisfied with their quarters, the three men left the house without payment, and on the old woman searching for them and finding them, they abused her roundly, on which she uttered this vow: 'May I be born in after years in such a condition as to kill you all three.'

[1] This may possibly refer to a "low-born king" (Pukkaśa) *vide supra*, p. 49.

Now," Buddha added, "these three men killed by the cow were these three merchants, and the cow itself was the old woman," and then he uttered these verses:

"From evil and abusive words and an overbearing, insulting disposition towards others, hatred and resentment increase and grow. Restraining one's words, and behaving decorously to men, using patience and courtesy, these evil consequences are self-destroyed. The future life of a man depends on his words, and therefore from evil words comes self-destruction."[1]

[On hearing these words Brimbasâra was filled with joy, and he and his followers departed.]

[1] Or, "a tortured existence (body)."

SECTION IX.

TWIN VERSES.[1]

1. FORMERLY when Buddha was residing at Śrâvastî, the king of the country, whose name was Prasenajit, came to the place where Buddha was, and descending from his chariot, approached the Teacher with the deepest reverence, and invited him on the morrow to enter the city and partake of his hospitality, with a view to exhibit to the people the excellency of his person and doctrine, that they might believe on him.[2]

Buddha having consented, on the morrow entered the city with all his disciples, and having passed through the four cross streets of the town, he came to the place appointed and sat down. After finishing the meal, he began, on the request of the king, to preach in the midst of the four highways,[3] whilst his auditors were very many. At this time there were two merchants listening to him. One of them reflected, "What excellent wisdom on the part of the king to have such doctrines as these publicly preached! how wide their application, how searching their character!"

The other reflected thus, "What folly is this on the part of the king, bringing this man here to preach! Like the calf that follows the cow, here and there, fastened to a vehicle she draws, bleating as it goes—so is this Buddha

[1] Here we come into agreement with the division of chapters in the Pâli. This chapter is called "Yamakavaggo," *i.e.*, "double verses." It agrees in title with K. xviii. Cod. iii.

[2] A similar story is told in the Chu'h Yau, Cod. iii. book 19, fol. 6.

[3] This preaching and begging in the "four highways" is constantly referred to in Buddhist works.

following the king." The two merchants having departed from the city some thirty li, came to an inn where they put up. In taking some wine the good merchant was restrained and protected by the four guardian spirits that watch over the world. The other, on the contrary, was incited by an evil spirit to drink on, till he was overpowered by sleep, and lay down in the road near the inn. Early in the morning, the merchants' waggons leaving the place, the drivers not perceiving the man lying in the road, he was crushed to death by the waggon wheels.

[The other merchant, having come to a distant country, was selected by the genuflection of a sacred horse[1] to succeed the king; and he accordingly was appointed to the throne. After this, considering the strange turn events had taken, he returned and invited Buddha to visit him, and preach to his people—on which occasion the World-honoured one declared the reason of the death of the evil-minded merchant, and the prosperity of him who thought wisely, and then added these lines]:

"The mind is the origin of all that is;[2] the mind is the master, the mind is the cause.[3] If in the midst of the mind[4] there are evil thoughts, then the words are evil, the deeds are evil, and the sorrow which results from sin follows that man, as the chariot wheel follows him (or *it*) who draws it.

[1] This reference to a "sacred horse" is curious. It seems to show some connection of Buddhism with Sun-worship.

[2] In the Chu'h Yau (Cod. iii.) this verse occurs under the heading of "Thought," K. xix. fol. $\frac{6}{1}$.

[3] This translation differs from the Pâli. All the Chinese versions, however, are agreed, and no other rendering seems to be admissible—"The mind is supreme, the mind is the cause." The latter term "shi" seems to agree with the Pâli "manomayo," "springing from the mind" (Ch. *sub. voc.*), whilst the Chinese "tsun" corresponds with "seṭṭho" (best, excellent, &c.)

[4] The Chinese "chung sin," although irregular, seems to be a close version of the Pâli "manasá." The question arises whether in these translations the construction is not adapted to the original, in opposition to strict rules.

The mind is the origin of all that is; it is the mind that commands, it is the mind that contrives. If in the mind there are good thoughts, then the words are good and the deeds good, and the happiness which results from such conduct follows that man, as the shadow accompanies the substance."

On hearing these words, the king and his ministers, with countless others, were converted, and became disciples.

2. In days of old, at the back of the Gridhrakûta mountains, near Râjagriha, there was a village, of some seventy or so families, all of them Brahmans. Buddha wishing to convert these people, came to the place and sat down under a tree. The people seeing the dignity of his presence, and the glorious appearance of his body, flocked round him, on which he asked the Brahmans how long they had dwelt in the mountain there, and what their occupation was. To this they replied—"We have dwelt here during thirty generations past, and our occupation is to tend cattle." On asking further as to their religious belief, they said—"We pay homage and sacrifice to the sun and moon, the rain (water), and fire, according to the several seasons. If one of us dies, we assemble and pray that he may be born in the heaven of Brahma, and so escape further transmigrations." Buddha replied to this—"This is not a safe way, nor by it can you escape from the three evil ways of further existence. The true way is to follow me, become true ascetics, and practise complete self-composure with a view to obtain Nivâna;" and then he added these lines:

"They who consider truth as that which is untrue,[1] and regard that which is untrue as truth,

[1] This corresponds with v. 11 of the Pâli. The Chinese "chin" is always used for "Truth," and, therefore, the Pâli "sāro" is in agreement (but it may also correspond with "*essentia.*" F.)

this is but to adopt heretical opinions,[1] and can never lead to true advantage. But to know as truth that which is true, and to regard as false that which is false, this is perfect rectitude, and this shall bring true profit. Everywhere in the world there is death—there is no rest in either of the three worlds. The Devas, indeed, enjoy a period of bliss; but their happiness also must end, and they must also die! To consider this as the condition of all states of being (worlds), that there is nothing born but must die, and, therefore, to desire to escape birth and death, this is to exercise one's self in Religious Truth."

The seventy Brahmans hearing these words, desired at once to become Shamans; and on being welcomed by Buddha, their hair fell off, and they presented the appearance of true disciples. Then they all set out to return to the Vihâra, and on the road certain thoughts about their wives and families troubled them, whilst at the same time a heavy downpour of rain prevented their advance. Then Buddha, knowing their thoughts, caused some ten houses to appear by the road-side, in which they sought shelter; but on entering one of them it was soon perceived that through the roof the rain found its way, and there was but little protection from the wet, on which Buddha added these lines, and said:

"As when a house-roof is not properly secured,[2] then the rain finds a way through it and drops within, so when the thoughts are not carefully controlled, the desires (sexual desires) will soon bore

[1] Or "this is but an erroneous view of the case" (*falsi studii participes*, F.)

[2] In the Pâli, v. 13, ss. The agreement is very close.

through all our good resolutions. But as when a roof is well stopped then the water cannot leak through, so by controlling one's thoughts, and acting with reflection, no such desires can arise or disturb us."

The seventy Brahmans, on hearing these lines, although convinced that their desires were reprehensible, yet were not wholly free from doubt, nevertheless they went forward.

As they advanced they saw some scented paper on the ground, and Buddha took the opportunity of calling their attention to it; and after this, seeing some fish-gut also lying about, he directed their notice to its ill-odour, and then added these lines, and said:[1]

"He who consorts with the low and the base, contracts the same character as he who handles a foul substance; he goes from worse to worse, and utterly without reason, he perfects himself in wickedness. But the wise man (consorting with the wise) contracts the same character, even as the scent of a sweet odour adheres to him who handles it; advancing in wisdom, practising virtue, he goes on to perfection, and is satisfied."

The seventy Brahmans, hearing these verses, convinced that their desire to return home and enjoy personal indulgence was the evil taint that adhered to them, cast off such thoughts, and, going forward, came to the Vihâra, and finally obtained the condition of Rahats.

3. In former days, when the nobleman Sudatta had bought of the heir-apparent, Jeta, the ground for a Vihâra, at Śrâvastî, then the said nobleman had invited Buddha

[1] This agrees with the story of Nanda ("Romantic Legend," p. 376).

and his followers to partake of his hospitality for a month, in consequence of which, and the sermons which the World-honoured then preached, all those present obtained enlightenment, and the Prince himself returned with joy to the Eastern Palace.[1]

Now Virudhaka, the prince's brother, was always near the person of the king; and on this occasion his majesty, with his suite, and the officers of the "after palace," proceeded to robe themselves, with the intention of visiting Buddha. Having arrived at the place where he was, they paid him the customary reverence, and with undivided attention listened to his instruction.

Meantime Virudhaka, remaining behind, was invited by the courtiers, in the absence of his father, to occupy his throne; and once seated there, he was unwilling to retire from it. [The consequence was, he sent and caused his father, and 500 of his followers, to be put to death. On which Buddha recited these lines]:

"The man who causes joy now, shall rejoice hereafter. Living virtuously, he doubly rejoices—he rejoices and is glad; seeing his own happiness, his heart is at rest. He rejoices now, he rejoices hereafter; doing right, he has a double joy; he enjoys Divine protection (here), and he receives his reward and is at rest (hereafter)."[2]

And then Buddha having foretold that Virudhaka, after seven days, should go down to hell, added these words:

"He who causes sorrow suffers sorrow hereafter. Walking in sin he doubly suffers—reflecting on the evil he has done, he suffers; seeing his guilt, he

[1] The Eastern Palace is alluded to by Fa-hien, and also in General Cunningham's Arch. Survey of India (*passim*).

[2] These verses correspond with 16, ss., in the Pâli.

suffers more in prospect of the future. The man who repents (mourns) now, repents hereafter. On account of his evil deeds he mourns in both worlds; seeing his own evil works, he endures the grief consequent on guilt (in this world), and he inherits the misery of his evil deeds (in the next)."

Buddha having addressed the people and the Prince Jeta at further length, on the folly of covetousness and an evil ambition, and Virudhaka having, as the prediction went, fallen into the condition of a lost man, the whole assembly was convinced, and were brought to a knowledge of the truth.

SECTION X.

ON CARELESSNESS (THOUGHTLESSNESS).[1]

1. In days of old there were five hundred merchants, who, after a voyage on the deep, were returning to their homes, when in traversing certain deep and dangerous passes the evil spirits so bewildered them that, being unable to find their way out, they at last were exhausted from want of food and lay down and died, leaving their treasures scattered about the mountains. At this time a certain Shaman, who was practising austerities in that neighbourhood, seeing the valuables lying about, thought thus with himself—"I have been exercising myself in self-denial for these seven years past, and have failed to reach my aim. I will take these valuables and go home again." Then Buddha, recognising the condition of this Shaman, and knowing that he would arrive at deliverance, caused the appearance of a Bhikshunî, with a head-dress adorned with jewels. On seeing her, the Shaman was astonished, and said, "How is it that you, a Bhikshunî, are thus adorned?" To which she replied, "But how is it that you, a Shaman, are also in possession of wealth and jewels, which are forbidden to one of your calling?"—and then she added these lines, and said:

"A Bhikshu diligently adheres to the rules (of his calling). A man who is careless and negligent in these, accumulates much sorrow. He who care-

[1] As I have observed in the Preface, the title of this chapter in Cod. iii. is "Reflection," agreeing with the Pâli.

fully attends to little matters, arrives at great results; he who accumulates evil actions must enter the fiery pit. But guarding the precepts, then one's happiness increases, and the gladness consequent upon it, as the contrary neglect of them leads to remorse and bitterness of heart. The Bhikshu who is able to get rid of all remnants of worldly attachment (the three worlds), this one is verily near to Nirvâna."

Then the Bhikshunî re-appearing in the glorious form of Buddha, the Shaman, filled with astonishment and fear, fell down at his feet, and repenting of his carelessness and ignorance, vowed to amend his life and follow his duty with anxious care. On this the World-honoured one forthwith recited these gâthâs:

"Although a man may have heretofore been careless, yet if afterwards he is able to govern and restrain himself, this man becomes illustrious in (or illumines) the world, and the more he reflects the more resolved will he become (to use self-restraint). A man may have done many things wrong, but if he recovers himself and atones for the evil by doing good, this man becomes illustrious in the world, and the more he reflects the more virtuous he will become. The man who in the prime of life leaves his home and perfectly tutors himself in the doctrine of Buddha, this man shines out in the world as the moon when it bursts from a cloud. The man who in times past has done wickedly, but afterwards halts in his career and offends no more—that man shines out in the world as the moon when it emerges from the cloud."

On hearing these lines, the Shaman again prostrated himself at the feet of Buddha, and returning to his solitary seat underneath a tree, applied himself sedulously to practise self-government and contemplation, and thus recovered the ground he had lost, and attained the fruit of Rahatship.

SECTION XI.

THOUGHT (CITTAVAGGO).

1. In times of old, when Buddha dwelt in the world, there was a certain religious person who had taken his abode under a tree beside the bank of a river. After practising himself in religious exercises for twelve years, he was still unable to get rid of worldly thoughts, or to banish recollections of worldly pleasures—to wit, those resulting from sight, or hearing, or smelling, or tasting, or handling, or thoughts about the properties of things around him (dharma) —and thus after these twelve years he was still unconverted. Buddha, perceiving his capability of conversion, transformed himself into a Shaman, and came to the tree where he sat, and occupied a place near the other. After a while, in an interval of moonshining, lo! they saw a tortoise come up out of the river, and come towards the tree; at the same time a hungry river-dog[1] coming along endeavoured to lay hold of the tortoise to eat him. But no sooner did he make the attempt than the tortoise, gathering up his head and tail and legs into his shell, was in perfect safety, and the dog could do him no harm. But no sooner had the dog gone on than the tortoise, emerging from his concealment, walked on again as before. On this the ascetic observed to the Shaman—"This tortoise, because it possesses such a safe protection (*lit.* 'a casque of salvation'), the dog was disappointed of his meal." To which the Shaman replied—"I remember a man who was very different from this. This man, forgetting the im-

[1] Otter?

permanency of all earthly things, and indulging in the six pleasures of sense, fell an easy victim to Mâra;[1] his body dissolved, his spirit[2] gone, he was whirled again through the endless forms of repeated births, a victim of the sorrows and the misery formed by his ill-regulated thoughts; and then he repeated these gâthâs:

"This body of thine shall soon return to the earth—your form destroyed, your spirit fled—why, then, covet such an abode? It is the mind that makes its own dwelling-place; from earliest time, the mind reflecting on evil ways, itself courts its own misery. It is the very thought that itself makes (its sorrow). Not a father or mother can do so much;[3] if only the thoughts be directed to that which is right, then happiness must necessarily follow. Concealing the six appetites as the tortoise conceals his limbs, guarding the thoughts as a city is surrounded by the ditch, then the wise man in his struggle with Mâra shall certainly conquer, and free himself from all future misery."

Then the Bhikshu, having heard these words, putting away all lustful desires, attained Rahatship, and recognising Buddha in the form of the Shaman, he prostrated himself at his feet; and all the Devas, Nâgas, and Spirits, who surrounded the spot, were filled with unutterable joy.

[1] Mâra the Tempter (in whatever sense).

[2] Shin=spirit or "soul."

[3] These stanzas correspond with 40 ss. of the Pâli. This story of the tortoise occurs throughout all the versions.

SECTION XII.

FLOWERS (PUPPHAVAGGO).

1. In days of old, when Buddha was residing at Śrâvastî, there was to the south-east of that country, in the mid-ocean, a certain islet (a mound, or fort, or look-out), on the top of which was a tree that bare beautiful scented flowers.

In the same spot dwelt five hundred women of the Brahman caste, wholly devoted to their worldly duties, ignorant that there was a Buddha born in the world. Now these women were in the habit of conversing together on the unhappiness of their worldly condition, and in consequence they used to go to the tree that surmounted their abode, and pluck the flowers and offer them to Brahmâ-deva, with the prayer that they might escape the power of Yama, and be born in heaven (Brahma-heaven). Now Buddha, perceiving their case, and knowing that they had the capacity of being converted, suddenly transported himself with his followers to their place of abode, and then came and sat down near them. The women seeing the wonderful sight, were lost in amazement, and exclaimed, "Brahmâ himself has come to answer our prayers!" But on this a certain Deva answered them, and said, "This is not Brahmâ, but the World-honoured Buddha, who has come to save the world." On this the women bowed down in reverence, and addressed Buddha in these words—"We, indeed, are but women, much polluted, yet we desire, above all things, to escape the power of Yama, and to be born in the highest heaven;" to whom Buddha replied, "May you, indeed, obtain your desire!

But there are two things in the world which are immutably fixed—that good actions bring happiness, and bad actions result in misery. But (it is not generally known that) the joys of heaven as well as the sorrows of earth are both to be avoided. Who, then, is able to pluck and to hold the true joy of perfect rest (the rest of non-action)? Truly ye have understanding, O women!" and therefore he recited these gâthas:

"Who is able to select (conquer ?)[1] the earth (*i.e.*, the place of his abode), to escape Yama,[2] and lay hold of heaven? Who (is able) to repeat the verses of the Law as one who selects choice (excellent) flowers? The enlightened (one) selects the earth, avoids Yama, seizes heaven, illustriously repeats the verses of the Law, is able to cull the flowers of virtue. Knowing that the world is like a hillock of sand,[3] that it is unsubstantial as a mirage, he separates the flowery arrows of Mâra,[4] and escapes from the necessity of birth and death.[5] Regarding the body as a bubble, as a self-created mirage, he separates the flowery garland of Mâra, and escapes from birth and death."

And so the 500 women were converted, and, in reply to Ânanda, Buddha explains how these women had formerly lived in the time of Kâśyapa Buddha, and because of their devotion to him, were now privileged to live in the time of Śâkya Buddha, and to be converted by him. And so on another occasion Buddha recited these gâthas:

1 This is expressed by a difficult passage. The Chinese *tseh* means "to select" or "pick out," and the whole verse seems to allude to choosing "a future abode" (bhûmi).

2 The expression "lam" in Chinese could hardly have been understood (as a proper name) except by the Pâli translation.

3 Like "froth" (Pâli), v. 46.

4 Instead of *foo* I have been obliged to substitute *tsin*, an *arrow*.

5 Probably the word *sing* is a mistake for *wang*, "King of Death."

"As many kinds of flowers when waived to and fro scatter their scent far and wide,[1] so wide is the renown of his accumulated merits, who once is born and lives as he ought. The scent of the Vassikî flowers does not travel against the wind, but the (odour) of those who live religiously spreads far and wide—the fame of the virtuous man pervades all places. The scent of sandal-wood and the Tagara,[2] of the Lotus and Vassikî flower, although real and sensible, is not as the fragrance of (him who walks according to) the precepts. Mean and false in comparison is the scent of the rarest flowers with the fame of him who holds by virtue, the excellency of whose conduct rises to heaven. He who thus lives in perfect agreement with the precepts, who walks circumspectly, and who by fixed thought has obtained release, he has far out-distanced the way of Mâra."

And on another occasion, when Buddha was residing on the Gridhrakûta Mountain, near Râjagriha, he recited the following gâthas:

"As a ditch[3] in the field, close beside the highway, will produce the lily in its midst, and spread far and wide its delightful perfume, so in the midst of life and death (that is, the phenomenal world), beside the way of false speculation (universal inquiry), the wise man diffuses his glad sentiments in becoming a disciple of Buddha."

[1] Agreeing with v. 53 (the Southern version). It is possible that the symbol "*to*" in the text ought to be translated "Tagara."

[2] Notice should be taken of the symbols used for Vassikî and Tagara.

[3] Pâli, v. 58, 59, vv.

SECTION XIII.

THE FOOL (BALAVAGGO).

I. ON a certain occasion, when Buddha was residing at Śrâvastî, there was a certain rich Brahman, eighty years old, who had built himself a large house, in ignorance of the impermanency of earthly things, in prospect of a long life. Buddha sent Ânanda to this man, and knowing that his death was near, he inquired why he had built such a house with so many apartments; and on the man giving his reasons, and explaining the several purposes of the numerous chambers, then the World-honoured repeated these gâthâs:

"'I have children and wealth,' such is the constant thought of the fool. He is not even his own master (or, himself)—what, then, are his children and his money? If it is hot, it will be so; if it is cold, it will be so. Many are the anxieties of the foolish man, but yet he knows nothing of the changes of the future. The fool who knows not his extreme folly yet claims knowledge; the fool who says he is wise is foolish indeed."

On the old man returning to his dwelling, he suddenly fell dead from a blow received as he walked, on which Buddha repaired to the place, and for the sake of the other Brahmans recited these verses:

"A fool, though he live in the company of the

wise, understands nothing of the true doctrine, as a spoon tastes not the flavour of the soup. The man of discernment, frequenting the society of the wise, in a moment perceives the secret of the true doctrine, as the tongue perceives the flavour of the broth. Even the charity of the fool is a cause of sorrow to him; how much more his evil deeds! That deed is ill done that causes repentance hereafter; the reward of which is accompanied by tears and a rueful face."

On hearing these lines the Brahmachârins were converted, and worshipping Buddha, arose and departed.

On another occasion, when a Pratyeka Buddha, called Kâla, entered Nirvâna, after enduring the insults of certain women as he begged his food, the World-honoured uttered these verses:

"The fool and his fellows[1] doing evil are unable to deliver themselves. Misfortune follows them with its certain burning. Their evil deeds must result, when they are completed, in entire destruction. The fool, whilst in the flesh, recognises not the misery he is entailing on himself; but when he sinks into the place of perdition, then he knows his own folly."

[1] *Yu ch'hwang*, which may mean simply the "stupid."

SECTION XIV.

THE WISE MAN (PANDITAVAGGO).

1. THERE was in old time a Brahmachârin just twenty years of age, who, being possessed of brilliant talent, foolishly thought that he could be instructed in no art or accomplishment common in the world. Taking his travels, therefore, he came to a country where he saw a fletcher making his arrows and shaping his bow; on seeing which he was convinced of his ignorance in this respect; and so also in another country, seeing a man building a ship, he was equally convinced; and so again when in another place he saw a man making a royal palace. Having learnt all these arts, and passed successively through sixteen countries, he came back to his own place, and boastfully asked, "Who is there in the world more acquainted with the arts than myself?"

Buddha perceiving his capacity for conversion, changed himself into a Shaman, and coming where he resided, with his robes orderly arranged, and his begging-dish in his hands, stood before him. "And who are you?" said the Brahmachârin. "I am a man able to govern his body," replied the Shaman. "And what is that?" inquired the other, on which the Shaman uttered these verses:

"The fletcher carves and adjusts the horn of which his bow is made; the pilot manages his ship; the architect hews his beams; the wise man governs his body (himself). For as, by way of simile, the solid rock is unshaken by the wind, so the wise man, grave of thought, quails not whether praised or blamed: just as a deep lake (is not easily stirred but remain) tranquil and still), so the wise man hearing the Law (way), his heart is quiet and at rest."[1]

The Shaman having recited these verses, by his supernatural power raised himself in the air, and exhibited the thirty-two superior signs of Buddha's person, on which the Brahmachârin was converted, and obtained the fruit of Rahatship.

2. In old times, when Buddha was residing in Śrâvastî, there was a village about 500 li off, in which dwelt some fifty or sixty families (mountain people). Amongst these there was a certain poor man and his wife, to whom had been born two boys (twins), very lovely to behold, and of incomparable grace. The one they called "Grace" (tih), the other "Fortunate" (fuh). Now it so happened one day the father had returned from his work, and lain down on his bed to rest, whilst the mother was still in the fields. The two children, who were then only seven or eight weeks old, not seeing their father, began to speak reproachfully one with the other, because they were born in such circumstances as they were, and had to fare so badly as they did. The father, overwhelmed with astonishment at hearing the children talking thus, and thinking that they were demons in human shape, resolved to kill them and burn their bodies. Accordingly, he went out into the fields to gather wood for the purpose, and meeting his wife he told her all about it. On this the mother, moved with pity, and scarce believing the truth of the matter, begged a respite for the children for a few days. On the morrow she herself went outside the dwelling and listened, when lo! she heard the children reproaching one another as before. On this, being persuaded that they were demons in children's form, she consented to the course usual in these cases, that they should be burned (either "burned alive," or "killed and burned"). At this time Buddha, knowing

[1] Compare vv. 80, 81 of the Pâli.

the circumstances of the case, transported himself to the village, and, resplendent with glory, lit up the place and all the surrounding country with the brightness of his presence. On this the villagers, and especially the parents of the children, came near to worship him. On seeing the parents, and hearing their account of the children, Buddha smiled, and from his mouth proceeded the five-coloured rays that shone through heaven and earth, and then he related the history of the twins, how that they had been disciples of Kâśyapa Buddha, and were in a fair way to arrive at perfect deliverance, when by mutual conversation on heretical doctrines they had hindered their escape, and had continued to be born, at one time in high degree, at another time in poverty, and at last as the twins of the poor people before him; and then the World-honoured recited these gâthas:

"The great man is entirely free from covetous desire—he dwells in a place of light himself enlightened. Although perchance he meet with sorrow, he rejoices;[1] without ostentation, he exhibits his wisdom. The wise man (bhadra) concerns himself with no worldly business; he desires neither wealth, children, or possessions (land), always carefully observing the precepts, and walking in the way of supreme wisdom, he hankers not after strange doctrine (or wealth or honour). The wise man, knowing the character of instability,[2] as a tree in the midst of sand (uses every effort) to change his friend whose mind is unfixed, and to bring him back from impurity to virtue (purity)."

On hearing these lines, the children were able to enter as Samaneras into the assembly, and the parents and other villagers entered the paths.

[1] Or, although perchance he has sorrow or joy.

[2] Or, knowing one of unstable character.

SECTION XV.

THE RAHAT (ARAHANTAVAGGO).

1. In old time there was a country called Na-lai (Nara), near the Southern Sea, in which the people gained their livelihood by seeking for pearls and selling sandal-wood. It happened that there were two brothers in this country, whose parents being dead, they agreed to separate and seek their several fortunes. One of them had a slave called Fun-na (Pûrna) of very quick intellect, who went out on his journey to seek for some profitable adventure for his master. Having made considerable gain by the sale of some ox-head sandal-wood, he came to Śrâvastî, and meeting with Buddha, was converted and became a Rahat. Returning then to his own people, and exhibiting before them the wonderful powers he possessed—viz., of ascending into the air, and causing water and fire to proceed from his person—he led many of them to become disciples, and finally, at their entreaty, Buddha himself came to convert the King, on which occasion the World-honoured uttered these stanzas:

"His[1] mind having been quieted, his words and deeds are also at rest; freed by the truth, in perfect peace he returns to (or finds refuge in) Nirvâna. Free from desire, without entanglements, released from the impediments of the world (three worlds), all thoughts of self-indulgence gone, this man is

[1] Compare vv. 96, 98, 99 of the Pâli.

rightly called Superior. Whether in the hamlet or in the wilderness, on the level land or the high bank of the river, wherever such persons dwell there cannot but be delight. They have found their delight in the wilderness, where men find none; passionless they rejoice, having no ground left for pleasure-seeking."

SECTION XVI.

THE THOUSANDS (SAHASSAVAGGO).

1. IN old time, when Buddha was residing at Śrâvastî, there was an old mendicant called Pan-teh-san (Patisena ?) who being by nature cross and dull, could not learn so much as one Gâthâ by heart. Buddha accordingly ordered 500 Rahats day by day to instruct him, but after three years he still was unable to remember even the one Gâthâ. Then all the people of the country (the four orders of people) knowing his ignorance, began to ridicule him, on which Buddha, pitying his case, called him to his side, and gently repeated the following stanza :—"He who guards his mouth, and restrains his thoughts, he who offends not with his body, the man who acts thus shall obtain deliverance." Then Patisena, moved by a sense of the Master's goodness to him, felt his heart opened, and at once he repeated the stanza. Buddha then addressed him further—"You now, an old man, can repeat a stanza only, and men know this, and they will still ridicule you, therefore I will now explain the meaning of the verse to you, and do you on your part attentively listen."

Then Buddha declared the three causes connected with the body, the four connected with the mouth, and the three connected with the thoughts, by destroying which men might obtain deliverance, on which the mendicant, fully realising the truth thus explained, obtained the condition of a Rahat.

Now, at this time there were 500 Bhikshunîs (Nuns) dwelling in their Vihâra, who sent one of their number to

Buddha to request him to send them a priest to instruct them in the Law, on which Buddha desired the old mendicant Patisena to go to them for this purpose. On hearing that this arrangement had been made, all the nuns began to laugh together, and agreed on the morrow, when he came, to say the Gâthâ wrong (backward), and so confuse the old man and put him to shame. Then on the morrow when he came, all the Bhikshunîs, great and small, went forth to salute him, and as they did so, they looked at one another and smiled. Then sitting down, they offered him food. Having eaten and washed his hands, they then begged him to begin his sermon. On which the aged mendicant ascended the elevated seat, and sitting down, began: "Sisters! my talent is small, my learning is very little. I know only one Gâthâ, but I will repeat that and explain its meaning. Do you listen with attention and understand." Then all the young nuns began to attempt to say the Gâthâ backwards; but lo! they could not open their mouths; and filled with shame, they hung down their heads in sorrow. Then Patisena having repeated the Gâthâ, began to explain it, head by head, as Buddha had instructed him. Then all the female mendicants hearing his words, were filled with surprise, and rejoicing to hear such instruction, with one heart they received it, and became Rahats.

On the day after this the King Prasenajit invited Buddha and the whole congregation of priests to assemble at his palace (and partake of hospitality). Buddha therefore recognising the superior and reverend appearance of Patisena, desired him to bear his alms-dish and follow him as he went. But when they came to the palace-gate, the porter, knowing his character (antecedents), would not let him go into the hall; for "We have no hospitality," said he, "for a priest who knows but one Gâthâ; there is no room for such common fellows as you—make place for your betters and begone." Patisena accordingly sat down outside the door.

Buddha having now ascended the dais, after having washed his hands, lo! the arm of Patisena, with the alms-dish in its hand, entered the room. Then the King, the ministers, and all the assembly, seeing this sight, were filled with astonishment, and said—"Ah! what arm is this?" On which Buddha replied, "It is the arm of Patisena, the mendicant. He has but just obtained enlightenment, and I desired him to bear my alms-dish behind me; but the porter has refused him admission, and so his arm has appeared with my begging-dish in the hand." On this he was admitted and entered the assembly. Then Prasenajit, turning to Buddha, said—"I hear that this Patisena is a man of small ability, and knows only one Gâthâ, how, then, has he obtained the supreme wisdom?" To whom Buddha replied—"Learning need not be much, conduct is the first thing. This Patisena has allowed the secret virtue of the words of this one Gâthâ to penetrate his spirit; his body, mouth, and thoughts have obtained perfect quietude; for though a man know ever so much, if his knowledge reach not to his life, to deliver him from the power which leads to destruction, what benefit can all his learning be?" and then Buddha repeated the following stanzas:

"Although[1] a man can repeat a thousand stanzas (sections), but understand not the meaning of the lines he repeats, this is not equal to the repetition of one sentence well understood, which is able when heard to control thought. To repeat a thousand words without understanding, what profit is there in this? But to understand one truth, and hearing it to act accordingly, this is to find deliverance. A man may be able to repeat many books, but if he cannot explain them what profit is there in this?

[1] Compare these verses with 102 ss. of the Pâli.

But to explain one sentence of the Law, and to walk accordingly, this is the way to find supreme wisdom (to become a Rahat)."

On hearing these words, two hundred Bhikshus obtained deliverance, and the King and his ministers were filled with joy.

2. In days of old, when Buddha was living in the Jetavana Vihâra, at Śrâvastî, preaching his doctrine, there was a certain rich Brahman of that country called Yamata, who was in the habit of asking all the Brahmans of the neighbourhood, upwards of 5000 men, to share in his hospitality, and receive gifts of cattle, slaves, clothes, money, &c., in the middle of every fifth year. On the present occasion, having received these gifts, and joined in the various sacrifices, they came to the place where Buddha was, flushed with joy and elated with pride. On this, Buddha, having reproved them for their folly, uttered the following stanzas:—

"If[1] a man each month repeat a thousand sacrifices, and go on making his bodily offerings without ceasing, this is not equal to that man's conduct who but for a moment, with undivided attention (*yih sin*, ekachittam), fixes his mind upon the Law. The happiness consequent on one moment of deep reflection exceeds that (which results from) of the sacrifice of the bodies (of untold victims). Although a man for a hundred years worship and sacrifice to the spirit of Fire, his merit is not equal to that of the man who for a moment pays reverence to the Three Holy Ones; the happiness consequent on one such act of homage excels that resulting from all those hundred years."

[1] Compare this with vers. 106, 107 of the Pâli.

On this, the World-honoured proceeded to address Yamata in the following words:[1]—

"There are four kinds of charitable offerings. What are the four? First, where the gifts are large, and the merit small; secondly, where the gifts are small, and the merit large; thirdly, where the gifts are large, and the merit large; fourthly, where the gifts are small, and the merit also small. And now, with respect to the first, when is the gift large, and the merit small? In the case of the foolish and deluded man who takes away life for the purpose of offering up sacrifices to the gods, accompanied by wine-drinking, singing, dancing, and the bestowal of wealth. Here the gifts are great, but the merit small indeed. With regard to the case when the gifts are small and the merit small, this is so when, from covetousness and an evil heart, the offerings given to the learned (or religious persons) are small and stint; in such case the reward also is stint. And when is it that the offerings, though small, entail a large reward? In the case when, from a principle of love, a man offers to a virtuous person (or religious man) what small gift he has, with a desire to learn from him the principles of true wisdom, this man reaps great reward. And lastly, the case of a great gift securing a great reward, as in the case of one who, realising the vanity of all earthly things, out of a good heart gives his wealth to found monasteries, or to purchase grounds for fruits, with which to make offerings to the Three Holy Ones, or who gives

[1] The sermon which follows is not a part of Dhammapada, but is in prose.

clothing and other necessaries for this same purpose, his merit, like the waters of the five rivers which enter the ocean, is immeasurable, his reward returns into his own bosom many fold, as the return of the seed sown by the husbandman in land prepared for it."

Yamata and the rest having heard these words, were filled with joy, whilst the Devas and Spirits were enabled to enter on the first path. Five thousand Brahmachârins became disciples, whilst Yamata and the other householders accepted the five rules, and the King, ministers, and others, sought refuge in the three defences, and became lay disciples, and obtained the eyes of the Law (religious insight).

3. There was in old time a certain disorderly person living in Râjagriha, who neither reverenced his parents or paid respect to his superiors, but always had resort to sacrifice and worship of the sun and moon and fire when he went wrong, hoping thereby to get merit, and feel happy in himself; but notwithstanding all his bodily exercises, in worship and offerings, he found no peace, even after three years' incessant perseverance. He at length resolved to go to Śrâvastî to inquire of Buddha. Arrived there, and seeing the glory of his person, he fell down at his feet, and said how he was placed. Then Buddha explained the folly of animal sacrifice, and the uselessness of all such exercises where the heart was untouched, and there was no filial reverence or dutiful behaviour to those to whom it belonged; and in conclusion recited these Gâthâs:—

"To sacrifice to Spirits in order to find peace (merit), or, after this life expecting reward, his happiness is not one quarter of that man's who pays homage to the good. He who is ever intent on good conduct and due reverence to others, who always venerates old age, four happy consequences increasingly attend that man—beauty and strength, and life and peace."[1]

On hearing these words the man was filled with joy, and sought permission to become a disciple, and after a while attained the condition of a Rahat.

[1] Compare this with 109 of the Pâli, where *áyu* corresponds to Ch. *shau*, *vaṇṇo* to *sih*, *sukham* to *ngan*, and *balam* to *lih*.

SECTION XVII.

EVIL CONDUCT (PÁPAVAGGO).

1. In old time, when Buddha was residing at Râjagriha, he sent a Rahat called Sumanta (Su-man-teh) to the country of Ki-pin (Cophen, *i.e.*, Gandhâra) with some personal relics (hair and nail) for a tower-temple (*i.e.*, a temple connected with which was a relic tower or stûpa) in the Southern Mountains, where 500 Rahats constantly dwelt, and every morning and evening burnt incense and conducted worship. At this time there were in the same mountains 500 monkeys, who having seen these men at their prayers, immediately agreed between themselves to erect by the side of a neighbouring deep stream a relic tower of stone and wood in honour of Buddha. This they did, and above it placed the surmounting pole (Tee) [1] with banners and flags. Here they came to worship every morning and evening, even as the religious men of the neighbouring monastery did. Now it happened about this time, owing to the sudden rising of the river, that these monkeys were caught by the torrent, and being unable to escape were drowned. In consequence of their good deeds, however, they were born as Devas in the Trayastriñśas Heaven, where they had palaces, and clothes, and food according to their new condition. Reflecting, then, on

[1] The word *Tee*, as it is used to denote the surmounting ornament of the Buddhist Stûpa, is the same as the Burmese "Htee," which again is derived from the Pâli "Khetta," signifying "earths" or "worlds," referring to the worlds supposed to exist above our own, and over which Buddha rules. The Chinese "ts'ah," denoting the same thing, is derived from the Sanskrit "Kshetra" (same sense).

their former lives, they saw that they had been the monkeys who were lying drowned in the valley, and accordingly they descended to earth, and collecting scented wood and other necessaries, they made a funeral-pyre on which to burn the 500 bodies. Being observed by some heretical Brahmans who dwelt in the neighbourhood, practising their austerities, and having been asked by them the reason of their conduct, they explained the whole matter, in consequence of which the Brahmans were induced to go to Buddha to learn his system of religion—accompanied by the Devas. Arrived there, Buddha explained that the 500 monkeys who were drowned and reborn in Heaven had in a former birth been Brahman heretics, who had made ridicule of, and laughed at the conduct of a Shaman, who dwelt in those same mountains, and because of his activity in ascending and descending the crags whilst engaged in building a sacred tower, had called him "Monkey-foot." For this they had been born as 500 monkeys; but because of their good deed in erecting the small tower beside the stream, they had been now born as Devas. And then Buddha added these stanzas:

"Lightly to laugh at and ridicule another is wrong; he who has thus acted will certainly receive as his reward abundance of tears, according to the guilt or aggravation of his conduct."

On this the 500 Devas prostrated themselves in adoration, and the 500 Brahmans, being converted, became Rahats.

2. In old time, when Buddha was residing in the Jetavana at Śrâvastî, preaching for the benefit of gods and men, the Prince Koli having imprisoned his father and killed his elder brother, the heir to the throne, proclaimed himself King, and inaugurated his reign by the slaughter of thousands of the Śâkyas, on which occasion the World-honoured one, addressing Mugalin, said:

"Not[1] in the void of heaven, not in the depths of the sea, not by entering the rocky clefts of the mountains, in none of these places can a man by any means escape his destiny, the consequence of the evil he has done. All men are liable to sorrow and pain; none can escape old age and death. The virtuous man alone possessed of wisdom; the man who gives not way to busy thoughts (about life), for him alone there is no evil."

In consequence of this sermon, countless men who heard it were able to enter the paths.

[1] Compare ver. 127 of the Pâli.

SECTION XVIII.

PUNISHMENT (DAṆḌAVAGGO).

1. In days gone by there was a country called Kin-tai (Gandhâra ?), in which was a very old mendicant afflicted with a very loathsome disease, which caused him to pollute every place he occupied. Being in a certain Vihâra belonging to the place, no one would come near him or help him in his distress. On this Buddha came with his 500 followers, and obtaining all sorts of necessary utensils and warm water, they together visited the place where the old mendicant lay. The smell in the place was so offensive that all the Bhikshus were filled with contempt for the man; but the World-honoured causing Śakra-deva to bring the warm water, then with his own hand (diamond hand) began to wash the body of the mendicant and attend to his maladies. Then the earth shook, and the whole place was filled with a supernatural light, so that the King and his ministers, and all the heavenly host (Devas, Nâgas, &c.) flocked to the place, and paid adoration to Buddha. Having done so, they all addressed the World-honoured, and inquired how one so highly exalted could lower himself to such offices as these, on which Buddha explained the matter thus:

"The[1] purpose of Tathâgata in coming into the world is to befriend these poor and helpless and unprotected—to nourish those in bodily affliction,

[1] This and the following sections are introduced into the prose part of the text.

whether they be Shamans or men of any other religion (Tao-sse)—to help the impoverished, the orphan, and the aged—and by so doing, and persuading others so to do, the consequent merit is so great that all his former vows are hereby accomplished, and he attains the great goal of all life, as the five rivers when they are lost in the sea."

The King then asked as to the former condition of this old mendicant, and why he was born to so sad a lot, to whom Buddha replied:

"In days gone by there was a king called Evil-conduct (Pâpakamma ?), who governed his subjects with tyranny and oppression. He used to send out his officers to afflict the people, and with cruel lashes to extort from them all they could get. There was a certain man of eminence about to be whipped, when he begged for mercy as he was a disciple of Buddha. On this the officer laid the whip lightly on him; but, nevertheless, because of his evil deeds he was afterwards born in hell, and repeatedly as a beast, and at last as a man, but always miserably diseased. Now at that time the King was Devadatta, the executioner was this diseased monk, and the eminent man was myself; but because I was the one who begged for mercy, my lot is now to help this wretched man, as he had mercy on me."

And then he repeated the following lines:—

"He[1] who inflicts pain on the gentle and the good, or falsely accuses the innocent, this man will

[1] Compare ver. 137 ss. of the Pâli.

inherit one of these ten calamities—either a direct visitation from Heaven (by fire, wind, or water); or, if born, a deformed and diseased body; or some spontaneous fiery outbreak,[1] or loss of reason, or some false accusation, or some governmental difficulty, or a gradual loss of worldly substance, or alienation of relatives, or destruction of treasure (crops or grain) by fire or lightning; and when dead, a birth in hell. These are the ten."

The diseased monk hearing these words, convinced of sin, turned to Buddha and did him reverence, on which he arrived at the condition of a Rahat; and the King also and his followers, filled with joy, took on them the five precepts, and entered the Paths.

2. In days of old, when Buddha was residing in the Jetavana, at Śrâvastî, and preaching his doctrine for the benefit of men and gods, there were in a country to the eastward, called Uttaravati, a company of 500 Brahmans, who had agreed to go together to the residence of a certain Nirgrantha ascetic on the banks of the Ganges, who, by polluting himself with dirt, &c., aspired to the condition of a Rishi. On their way they were overtaken in the desert with thirst. Seeing a tree, and hoping to find some human habitation near, they hastened on to it, but when arrived there they found no sign of life; on this, they raised their voices in lamentation. Suddenly from the tree they heard the voice of the resident Spirit, who asked them why they lamented so, and on hearing the reason, supplied them to the full with drink and meat. The Brahmans, ready to start onward, asked the Spirit what had been his previous history, that he was thus born; on which he explained that having gone to the assembly of priests in Śrâvastî when Sudatta had bestowed the garden on Buddha, he

[1] I cannot translate this passage satisfactorily.

had remained all night listening to the Law, and having filled his drinking-cup with water as he went, had bestowed it in charity among the priests. On his return next morning, his wife in anger asked him what annoyance he had received that he should stop away all night. On which he replied that he was not annoyed, but he had been to listen to Buddha preaching at the Jetavana. On this his wife began roundly to abuse Buddha, and said, "This Gotama is but a mad preacher, who deceives the people," and so on. On this I resented not her statements, but rather submitted to them, and so when I came to die I was born as a spirit, but on account of my pusillanimity I was confined to this tree; and then he recited these verses:—

"Sacrifices and such services are sources of misery—day and night a continual burthen and anxiety; to escape sorrow, and destroy the elements of the body, a man should attend to the Law (of Buddha), and arrive at deliverance from all worldly Rules of Religion (world Rishis)."

The Brahmans having heard these words, resolved themselves to go to Śrâvastî, to the place where Buddha was, and having explained the object of their visit, the World-honoured recited these stanzas:—

"Although[1] a man goes naked with tangled hair, or though he clothe himself with a few leaves or garment of bark, though he cover himself with dirt and sleep on the stones, what use this in getting rid of impure thoughts?[2] But he who neither contends or kills, or destroys by fire, who

[1] Compare ver. 141 of the Pâli. [2] Or, folly.

desires not to get the victory, who is moved by goodwill towards all the world. There is no ground in such a case for ill-will or hate."

On hearing these words the Brahmans were converted, and became Shamans.

SECTION XIX.

OLD AGE (JARÁVAGGO).

1. BUDDHA was residing in the Jetavana, at Śrâvastî. After having eaten, he began to preach the Law of Eternal Life[1] for the benefit of gods and men, in the presence of the King and his ministers. At this time there were seven men, Brahmans, who had come from a distance, and having bowed at the feet of the World-honoured one, besought him to allow them to dwell near him, and hear his instructions. Having had the permission, they were assigned an upper chamber as their dwelling-place. Having retired there, they began to talk together and laugh loudly. On hearing this, Buddha went to them, and opened his mouth in these words :—

"What[2] (room for) mirth, what (room for) laughter, remembering the everlasting burning (or fire). Surely this dark and dreary (world) is not fit for one to seek security and rest in. Behold this body in its fashioning; what reliance can it afford as a resting-place, filled with crowded thoughts, liable to every disease. Oh! how is it men do not perceive its false appearances? When old, then its beauty fades away; in sickness, what paleness and leanness—the skin wrinkled, the flesh withered,

[1] "The Law of sweet dew" (amatam).

[2] This verse occurs in Cod. iii., K. I. fol. 9, under the heading of "Impermanence." Compare ver. 146 and ss. of the Pâli.

death and life both conjoined. And when the body dies, and the spirit flees, as when a royal personage rejects a (broken) chariot, so do the flesh and bones lie scattered and dispersed. What reliance, then, can one place on the body?"

On hearing these words, the Brahmans became sobered and thoughtful, and finally attained to the condition of Rahats.

2. In days of old, when Buddha was residing in the Jetavana, at Śrâvastî, preaching the Law for the good of Devas and men, at this time there was a Brahman village, consisting of some five hundred or more families, in which were also five hundred young Brahman students training themselves in the secret lore of their caste, and filled with disdain for all others, without any reverence for old age or superior rank. Now these five hundred youths, vaunting their own powers of investigating truth, spoke thus: "As for this Shaman Gotama, he does but self-style himself Buddha; his talents reach but little way compared with ours; we ought to challenge him to come here and dispute with us." Accordingly, they sent one to challenge him; and so Buddha, with all his disciples, came to the place, and having sat down beside some running water, they ate their food and washed their hands. At this time an old Brahman and his wife passed along through the village, begging their food. Buddha, knowing that formerly this old man had been very rich, and one of the chief ministers of the kingdom, he immediately turned to the young Brahmans, and asked them whether they knew who this old man was? They all answered at once, "We know perfectly." And then Buddha inquired again, "And who is he?" They said, "He was formerly a great minister, and very rich." "Then how is it (Buddha asked) he is now begging his food?" To which they replied, "Because he took no care of his money, and was foolish

in using it, he is now poor." Then Buddha said, "Brahmans! there are four things in the world difficult to do; those who can do them shall certainly obtain much happiness (merit), and escape poverty. And what are the four? First, when in the heyday of youth not to be disdainful; secondly, when advancing in years to give up thoughts about pleasure (sensual indulgence); thirdly, when rich, to be ever mindful of charity; fourthly, to give respectful attention to the words of a wise teacher. It is for want of observing these four rules that this old Brahman (gentleman) has come to his present condition, and is like an old stork sitting beside a dried-up pond. And then the World-honoured added these stanzas, and said:—

"To be constantly (morning and night) disdainful and supercilious, when old still to be lustful, having wealth to be niggardly, to reject the words of Buddha—these four propensities, what miseries do they bring; and, alas! when old age comes (how do they add to), the withered form and the worn-out appearance! The man who, when young, pleases himself, when old shall be trodden down. Not walking continently (in mature years), riches shall slip from him (when old)—even as the white stork that sits alone by the dried-up pool, so he who has disregarded the Rules of a Moral Life shall come to poverty. Old and feeble, with exhausted powers—what good can follow anxious thought. When old, like autumn leaves, decayed and without covering, life ebbed out and dissolution at hand, little good repentance then!"

And then Buddha added—"There are four opportunities given to every one who is leading a religious life, to attain deliverance and to avoid sorrow; and what are the four?

First, when young and capable of high moral resolves secondly, when rich and possessed of means; thirdly, when happy enough to gain the knowledge of the three honourable ones, and so have the opportunity of widening one's capabilities of merit; fourthly, when by experience a man has learned the vanity of earthly things, to act accordingly. Those who avail themselves of these opportunities will in the end certainly attain wisdom;" and then the World-honoured one added these stanzas:—

"Day and night, striving to get rid of fleshly desires, and at the right opportunity putting forth earnest effort; discovering the truth that all things are impermanent—such a man shall never fall into the pit of destruction. Aiming to learn how to kindle the lamp of reflection, and seeking in the light of experience supreme wisdom (prajñâ), removing all defilements, and avoiding pollution, by this light a man shall discover the ground of escape (Bôdhi)."

The World-honoured having uttered these words, caused the glory of his person to manifest itself, and in consequence the young Brahmans were convinced of his character, and besought permission to enter the church, and at length arrived at perfect deliverance (the condition of Rahats).

SECTION XX.

LOVING THE BODY (SELF) (ATTAVAGGO).

1. IN old time there was a country called To-mo-ho-lo (Damakara?), and about seven lis from the (chief) city there was a Vihâra, in which dwelt 500 Shamans. Amongst these was an aged mendicant named Mo-ho-lu (Makhara?), who, being of a heavy and dull mind, was unable to learn even one Gâthâ, though instructed by the 500 Shamans through many years. On this he was treated contemptuously by the rest, and not allowed to go in their company, but left to sweep the monastery, and look after the cells of the monks. On one occasion the King of the country had asked all the Shamans to assemble at his palace, and accept his hospitality. On this occasion, Makhara, having been left behind as usual, he thought thus with himself—"I have been born dull and stupid, and cannot even recollect one verse of Scripture. What use is it to live any longer, to be neglected and despised by my fellow-men?" On this he took a rope, and going to the back of the garden, he placed himself under a great tree intending to hang himself. At this time Buddha, by his power of religious discernment (eyes of religion), seeing the case of this man, transformed himself at once into the appearance of the Tree-Spirit, and with half his body[1] projecting from the tree, addressed the old monk in these words of

[1] This is constantly the sign of a supernatural appearance, as *e.g.*, in in Pl. xci. fig. 4, "Tree and Serpent Worship," where the Deva of the Bôdhi Tree, or the Vajrâsana under the Tree, is respectfully acknowledging the announcement of Buddha's birth, and, in so doing, reveals "half his body." [This scene is frequently referred to in Buddhist books.]

expostulation—"Psha! psha! thou (foolish) mendicant, what art thou going to do?" On this Makhara opened out the cause of his grief; on which the Tree-Spirit continued and said—"Do no such thing as this, but listen to my words: In the time of Kâsyapa Buddha, long ago, you were then a Shaman deeply acquainted with the three books (baskets—*i.e.*, Pitakas), and among your 500 brethren you were pre-eminent, in consequence of which you were filled with pride and self-complacency, and despised all others on account of their ignorance; and because you died then without repentance, it has been your lot ever since to be born dull and stupid—what good, then, to destroy yourself?"

And then Buddha, appearing in all his glory, added these verses:—

"If[1] a man love himself, let him carefully protect that which he is so anxious about (*i.e.*, himself). If he hope to be delivered from carnal desire, let him learn the right way without indolence (sleep). Himself, this is the first consideration; let him put forth his own power and attain wisdom. Profiting (himself in this way), he may then instruct others. Unwearied in his efforts, he will then gain wisdom. The enlightened man will first govern himself, then in due time he will be able to govern others. Regulating his own conduct (himself), and entering (on the domain of) true wisdom, he must necessarily ascend to the highest place (*i.e.*, become eminent). But if one cannot improve (profit) oneself, how can such an one benefit others; and, on the other hand, what desire (vow) may not be accomplished when oneself is able to lord it rightly over oneself? That

[1] Compare ver. 157 of the Pâli.

which I now do in my body, hereafter shall I myself receive; if I do evil, myself will cause the more, as the steel drill bores the gem."[1]

Makhara, on hearing these words, and seeing the glory of Buddha's appearance, immediately fell at his feet in worship, and was able to attain to peace. Moreover Buddha directed him to repair to the King's palace; and having preached there, he became a Rahat. [And the King and his ministers, &c., entered on the Paths.]

2. In days of old, when Buddha was residing at Śrâvastî, there were 500 Brahmans who continually sought to bring some railing accusation against him. Buddha, by his divine sight, penetrating their intention, and being moved by compassion towards them, desired to bring them to a knowledge of the truth. They had arranged between themselves to persuade a butcher to ask Buddha to receive his hospitality, and then, whilst he was there, to cause the slaughter of different creatures around him, so that in condemning slaughter, he must of necessity condemn his host, or, in praising his host, he must condone the slaughter. Then Buddha, having accepted his host's invitation, addressed him thus—"When the fruit is ripe it will fall of itself, so when merit is ripe, it will of itself exhibit itself (produce salvation)." Then the butcher, returning to his house, made all necessary preparations for the entertainment. At the appointed time Buddha arrived, and having mounted the preaching throne, he was moved by a strong desire to bring about the conversion of the Brahmans, and those assembled with them; and perfectly knowing their hearts, he began by causing his tongue to cover his face,[2] and his glory to appear through the whole city; and then he uttered the following stanzas:—

[1] Compare ver. 161 of the Pâli.

[2] This extraordinary sign is referred to in all Buddhist books, and is assumed to be the proof of strict truthfulness.

"The teaching of the wise[1] is this, that by wisdom we preserve ourselves. The foolish ridicule it —they see, and yet do wickedly; and so by their wicked deeds they reap misfortune, as he who sows the noxious plant (reaps the same). The wicked man in his own person accumulates (receives the fruit of his) guilt; the good man reaps good fruit (merit) in his own person; and so each one for himself prepares the harvest for himself. The concerns of another do not effect one's case—doing good, then we reap good, just as one who sows that which is sweet (enjoys the same)."[2]

On hearing these words, the Brahmans were convinced of their folly, and became disciples. The butcher also and his associates were converted, and then the All-Wise returned to the Vihâra.

[1] *Chin jin*, literally, a supernatural Being. The whole passage, therefore, might be rendered "as the teaching of supernatural (religion), is that by wisdom (*taou*), we may preserve life (or, our body), &c."

[2] This agrees generally with vers. 164, 165, of the Pâli.

SECTION XXI.

THE WORLD (LOKAVAGGO).

1. In days of old there was a certain Brahman King, whose name was To-mi-seay (Dhamasa?). It came into the heart of this King one day to distribute, according to the fashion of the Brahmans, an unlimited quantity of precious stones, &c., among the followers of his faith, the rule being that every Brahmachârin who came as a recipient (beggar) might take a handful from the heap and go. And so for many days the affair was conducted; and yet the pile of wealth did not appear to diminish. On this, Buddha, knowing the condition of the King, and his aptitude (capacity) for conversion, transformed himself into a Brahmachârin, and went to the spot. The King going out from his palace, when he beheld him approaching, paid him due respect, and conducting him within, inquired what he would desire to receive, and requested him to have no reserve in asking. On this the Brahmachârin replied, "I have come from far, and I desire to beg a few jewels, that I may have enough to build me a house." The King immediately answered, "Most virtuous sir, you may take a handful, and welcome." On this the Brahmachârin took so much from the heap, and then having gone seven paces, he returned and replaced them on the heap. On this the King inquired why he acted thus, in not taking the jewels. Whereupon the Brahmachârin replied, "This handful is indeed enough to enable me to build a house; but afterwards I shall want to take a wife, and for that purpose this handful is not sufficient." On this

the King bade him take three handfuls, and welcome. Having done so, and gone seven paces, again he returned and replaced the jewels on the heap. Whereupon the King once more inquired his reason for so doing, to which he replied, "These might be enough to provide me with house and wife, but then I shall have to buy slaves and oxen and horses, and for this purpose the three handfuls are not sufficient." On this the King said, "Take then seven handfuls, and welcome." The Brahmachârin having done so, and gone seven paces, again returned and did as before, saying that these seven handfuls, though enough for the purpose assigned, would yet not suffice for the maintenance and welfare of his children. On this the King bade him take the whole heap of jewels, and use them for the purposes named. Accordingly the Brahmachârin did so, and departed. On this the King, astonished, cried out to him in a loud voice what his reason for so acting might be? To which the man replied, that those who *begged* sought only things for the present life; whilst those who *thought*, found out the instability and impermanence of all worldly things, and the ever-accumulating mass of sorrow and pain that resulted from a worldly life. And on this, resuming his own glorious body as Buddha, he added these stanzas:—

"Though a man possessed a heap of jewels as high as heaven, enough to fill the world, not so happy he as one who apprehends the first principles of truth; he who makes vice resemble virtue, and love resemble hate (or, confuses the one with the other), he who confounds the true source of joy with sorrow—that man surely, bereft of reason, causes his own destruction."

Hearing these words, the King was filled with joy, and both he and his ministers received the precepts, and entered the Paths.

SECTION XXII.

BUDDHA (BUDDHAVAGGO).

1. In days of old Buddha was residing in Magadha, under the tree that overshadowed the Bodhimanda. Having by the power of his presence (virtue) overpowered Mâra, he was considering with himself that the five men whom formerly his father had sent to look after him,[1] and provide him with sufficient food, were in a condition to hear the sound of the drum of the Law of eternal life; and perceiving that they were at Benares, he immediately rose from underneath the tree, whilst the heaven and earth were lit up with a supernatural light, and the ground underneath him shook. Rejoiced at these indications, he went forward, and in the mid-road he encountered a Brahmachârin named Upaka (Yeon-fu), who had left his relations and home in search of a teacher to guide him in the way of truth. Beholding the World-honoured one, how reverend his appearance and joyous his mien as he went on the way, he cried to him with a loud voice, "O sir! full of religious thought and spiritual discernment, What is your history, and who has been your teacher, that you have arrived at such a condition as this?" To whom Buddha replied in the following stanzas:—

"Of myself, and by myself, have I attained to the eightfold Wisdom[2]—there is now nothing to

[1] This is a new idea, as far as I know, with reference to the five men. [The incident is referred to in a Chinese Life of Buddha called *Kwo-hu-in-tsai-yin-kwo*, Kiouen 3, f. $\frac{3}{2}$.]

[2] The Ashtângamârga *vide* "Eitel's Handbook," *sub* Mârga.

remove, nothing that defiles. All love of earthly things is at an end. I have destroyed the net of lust. Of myself, without any master, have I attained this position; nor need I now any protector or patron. Alone I stand, without any associate in conduct; having had this one aim, I have become Buddha (enlightened), and by this, have attained perfect holiness."

Upaka having heard these words, without any spiritual understanding, asked further, "Well, Gotama,[1] which way are you going?" To which Buddha replied, "I am going to Benares, to sound the drum of the insurpassable Law, which never yet has been heard, by which both Devas and men may attain Nirvâna, even as I now have attained." Then Upaka joyously replied, "Well said! sadhu! may you, as you say, be able to declare the Law of Eternal Life!" And having said so, Upaka turned away on another way, and so lost the chance of finding a teacher to guide him into the right way.[2] In the middle of that night Upaka died; on which occasion Buddha, perceiving the fact by his spiritual sight, spoke as follows (after a similar sentiment in prose):—

"Perceiving truth, pure and unalloyed, delivered from the five paths of destruction (five modes of birth), Buddha has come forth to enlighten the world, to make a way of escape from all sources of sorrow and pain. To be born as a man is difficult;[3] to attain to years (*i.e.*, to live long) is also difficult;

[1] We need scarcely remark that the epithet Gotama in the Northern Books is sometimes a mark of disrespect or indifference.

[2] For this story of Upaka, *vide* "Romantic Legend," p. 245.

[3] Compare ver. 182 of the Pâli, in which I think the expression, "*hard* is the life of man" (M. M.), may reasonably be changed into the "*difficult*," &c. This verse is found in the "Sûtra of Forty-two Sections."

to be born when Buddha is incarnate is difficult; and to hear the preaching of the Law of Buddha is difficult also."

On hearing these words, five hundred heavenly visitors were filled with joy, and entered the Paths.

2. In days of old there was a country about 4000 lis to the south of Râjagriha wholly given up to Brahmanic rites, with about a thousand Brahmans (or several thousands) as inhabitants. At a certain period there was a drought in that country, extending over a space of three years. In vain the people had made sacrifices to all their gods—no good resulted. At length the King asked the Brahmachârins how this happened; to which they replied, "We must observe the very utmost of the Law, and dismiss certain men to hold converse with Brahma Deva, and request an end of these calamities." On which the King demanded their intentions, with a view to forward them, to which they replied, "We require to have twenty chariots, with wood, incense, unguents, flags, and money, and sacrificing vessels." The King having provided these things, they departed from the city about seven lis, and there, on a level space of earth, they erected their wood on high, and then exhorted one another not to regard their present bodily condition, but to aspire to be born in the heaven of Brahma; and so at length seven men were induced to consent to ascend the pyre, and be burned upon it. Then, after the usual prayers and ceremonies, they mounted the wood, and awaited the end. But when the light was applied to the lower part, hearing the crackling sound, and affrighted by the prospect of death, they arose and ran here and there, and besought to be rescued—but all in vain; and then, in distraction, they prayed thus, "Oh, is there no one in the three worlds to pity us! Oh, come thou and rescue us!" Hearing these words, Buddha appeared in mid-air above them, and as they were filled with joy, he said:—

"Truly men seek (through fear) many a refuge; they resort to mountains and valleys, and spirits residing in trees; they erect images as gods, and pay religious worship to them, seeking happiness (merit).[1] But such refuge as this is neither fortunate or best; not one of them is able to save thee from sorrow (or accumulated pain). But he who takes refuge in Buddha, the Law, and the Church, and with clear insight penetrates the meaning of the four truths, he will certainly attain (see) supreme wisdom.[2] He who seeks personal refuge in these three, finds the most fortunate and the best. In these only, without other refuge, a man may find deliverance from all sorrow."

On hearing these words, the sound of fire was no longer heard, and the Brahmans and their attendants, as they beheld Buddha (who now appeared) in his glory, were filled with joy, and beholding his miraculous appearances, were converted, and, descending from the pyre, they uttered these words:—

"Oh, the happiness of seeing the Holy One! Oh, the happiness of being able to rely on him as present! Oh, the joy of the man who is able to avoid the company of the foolish, and act well and virtuously by himself! How happy he who scrupulously guards the path of truth (true perception, or true ways); happy he who can repeat the Law; happy he who avoids discussion (contention) in the

[1] Compare ver. 188 of the Pâli.

[2] I have accidentally omitted a verse. "By understanding the four truths, a man escapes from the extreme misery of repeated birth and death; and to escape the eight calamities of life is to get rid of the whole body of pain."

world; happy he who always observes the precepts; happy he who consorts with the good, and treats them as his own kith; he who frequents the company of the virtuous is a wise man, and of high renown."[1]

Having said these words, the seven men became Rahats, and the King and his ministers, with countless Devas, after entering the Paths, were privileged to see much rain descending on the land.[2]

[1] This last verse is difficult to translate. The phrase "*to-wan*" means either "celebrated" or "a disciple" (one who hears much).

[2] The preceding verses correspond generally with 194 and 195 of the Pâli.

SECTION XXIII.

REST AND REPOSE (SUKHAVAGGO).

1. In days of old about 300 lis to the south of Râjagriha there was a village of some 500 or so mountain peasants, whose hearts were estranged from religion, and beyond the usual means of conversion, and yet were not indifferent to the hope of final salvation. On this the World-honoured One, transforming himself into the appearance of a Shaman, went to the village to beg his food, and having gathered sufficient, he left the village and took his seat beneath a neighbouring tree. Whilst thus sitting he entered on a condition of Samâdhi called that of Nirvâna, and so continued for seven days, without moving, and (apparently) without breathing. The men of the village seeing him thus, and believing life to be extinct, said among themselves, "This Shaman is evidently dead; we will collect wood for a funeral pyre, and burn his body." Having done so, they set fire to the wood. After it had gone out Buddha arose from its embers, and manifesting his glorious body in various miraculous ways, he returned to the shade of the tree where he was before, and again seated himself in perfect composure. The villagers, seeing this wonderful occurrence, one and all came near and paid him reverential homage, and said, "We indeed are but poor mountain people, and did not know that you were a god, and therefore prepared the pyre to burn your body on. We confess our fault, and pray forgiveness, and supplicate that no misfortune may befall us in consequence, whether disease, or famine, or drought." On this

the World-honoured opened his mouth, and uttered these stanzas:—

"My life is now at rest, with no anger amongst those who are angry (or those who hate). Men indeed on all sides feel anger, but my life (conduct) is free from anger. My life is now at rest, free from disease amongst the diseased; all men suffer from disease, to me there is none. My life is now at rest, sorrowless in the midst of sorrow; all men have sorrow, but I have none. My life is now at rest, in perfect peace, without any personal aim (*wou wei*), feeding on (unearthly) joys, like the bright gods above (Abhâsvaras). My life is now at rest, calm, indifferent, with no thought about 'what I must do.' Pile up then the wood, and let the fire encircle me; but how can it touch such an one as I?"[1]

On this the villagers embraced the faith and became Rahats, and Buddha and his followers returned through the air to the bamboo grove, on which occasion the World-honoured explained to Ananda that in former days, when he had been a Pratyeka[2] Buddha, he had, underneath this same tree, obtained Nirvâna, and because the villagers had piously burnt his body, and collected his relics and placed them in a casket, and done reverence to them, they were now privileged to hear him preach, and so had obtained the fruition of the Paths. After this explanation, countless Devas obtained knowledge of the Paths.

2. In days of old, when Buddha was residing in the Jetavana, at Śrâvastî, there were four Bhikshus seated under

[1] Compare Max Müller's note (200) about the words of the King of Mithilâ.

[2] Observe that the Chinese phrase for Pratyeka is "pi-chi," evidently the translation of the Pâli or Mâgadhî "Pacce(ko)."

a tree, who conversed together thus: "What think you is the greatest misery to bear in all the world?" One said the greatest misery in the world is lust; another said the greatest misery is hunger and thirst; another said it was anger; another said it was fear. Whilst they were thus disputing, without any hope of agreement, Buddha, knowing the case, transported himself to the spot, and inquired what their disputation was about. On this the Bhikshus, having arisen and paid him homage, explained how the case stood. On this the World-honoured explained that they had not got to the bottom of the matter, but that the body itself was the greatest misery, for from the body comes the misery of hunger and thirst, cold and heat, anger, and pride, and lust; and therefore our aim should be to get rid of the body, and thus attain the perfect rest of Nirvâna. And then he added these stanzas:—

"There[1] is no burning greater than lust; there is no distress (poison) worse than hate; there is no misery greater than this body; there is no joy like (its) destruction. Without accordance there can be little joy; small power of distinguishing truth argues little wisdom; by perceiving and seeking for that which is truly great, by this means alone one obtains perfect rest. Now I, the Honoured of the World, fully explain the character of the sorrowless; I fully (am able) to deliver the three worlds; I alone (or by myself alone) have overthrown the whole army of Mâra (the devil)."

Having uttered these words, Buddha explained how that in ages gone by there was a certain Bhikshu possessed of the five supernatural powers (*iddhi*), who dwelt in the mountains under a tree, practising austerities with

[1] Compare ver. 202 of the Pâli.

a view to final release. Whilst dwelling thus, four animals also came and took up their abode near him, namely, a small bird (sparrow?), a large bird (quail?), a poisonous snake, and a deer. On one occasion the Bhikshu heard these creatures also contending between themselves which was the greatest misery in the world, and they also, from their various dispositions, assigned the same causes of suffering as you have, namely, lust, hunger, anger, and fear. Whereupon the Bhikshu explained to them also, as I have done to you, that the body, the source of all sorrow, is the greatest misery, and therefore the greatest happiness is to get rid of the body and obtain Nirvâna. And on this they were able to understand the truth. Now at that time I was the Bhikshu, and ye were the four creatures. On hearing this the mendicants were filled with holy fear and self-upbraidings, after which they were able to come to the condition of Rahats.

SECTION XXIV.

PLEASURE (PIYAVAGGO).

1. In days of old, when Buddha was residing in the Jetavana, Vihâra, at Śrâvastî, there were four newly-admitted mendicants who went together and sat under a plum-tree, intending to engage themselves in religious contemplation (dhyâna). At this time the tree was in full bloom, and struck by the beautiful colours and the fragrant perfume of the blossoms, the conversation of the mendicants took the following turn—viz., as to what in all the world was most worthy of love as a source of pleasure. Then one of them said, "I think the greatest happiness in the world is during some moonlight night in spring, when all the trees are in bloom, to wander forth in the country, and take one's pleasure without constraint." Another said, "I think the highest pleasure is in joining in some family social gathering, and enjoying the feast and the wine, the music and the dancing." Another said, "I think the highest happiness is to possess such funds of wealth as to enable one to procure whatever the heart desires, whether it be chariots or horses, clothing or ornaments, such as would make one, on going into the world, the admiration and envy of all beholders." The fourth said, "And I think the highest happiness to be to possess a wife as beautiful as possible, and to see her clad in all the choicest robes, anointed with the rarest unguents, and always ready for the indulgence of love." Now Buddha, perceiving that these men were capable of conversion, but had not yet arrived at a knowledge of the impermanency of

the six objects of desire, immediately, with a sigh, addressed the four men, and asked them, "What is the subject of your discourse, as you sit here together beneath this tree?" On this they told him truthfully what each one's idea of happiness was. And then Buddha rejoined, "Let there be an end of such discourse, for all these things (which you desire) are the causes of (way of) sorrow, misfortune, fear, and calamity. This is not the way of eternal peace, the system of the highest joy. The flowers of spring shall fade in autumn, and fall in utter decay before the winter cold. All those friends in whose society you place such reliance for happiness, ere long shall be scattered and separated far and wide. That wealth you prize, and that beauty of wife, and those pleasures, alas! are the causes of every misfortune—hatred in families, wreck of body, future misery! Wherefore, O Bhikshus! be sure that the highest bliss is to leave the world, to search after supreme wisdom, to covet a condition of entire indifference, to desire nought for one's self, to aim at Nirvâna." And then the World-honoured uttered these stanzas:—

"From[1] love (or lust) comes sorrow, from lust comes fear; where there is no lust (or, no ground for lust), what sorrow, what fear can there be? From pleasure comes sorrow, from pleasure comes fear; where there is no ground for pleasure, what grief or fear can there be? From covetousness (greed) comes sorrow, from greed comes fear; where one is free from covetousness, there can be no sorrow or fear. But to be greedy to fulfil perfectly the requirements (moral rules) of the Law—to be truthful in everything (or, to be perfectly truthful), to be modest in everything, to conduct his own business (to order himself) according to what is right—this

[1] Compare vers. 212, 213, ss. of the Pâli.

is to lay a foundation of love from all. The idea of pleasure not yet produced, his thoughts and words composed, his mind unaffected by any bewilderment of love, he indeed shall mount above (or cut off) the Stream."[1]

[Having uttered these words, Buddha explained that in days gone by there was a King who, having entertained four other neighbouring Kings, and indulged them in every pleasure, similar questions to the above arose amongst them, and at last the King who was the host explained the matter as Buddha had done, on which occasion the four Kings were the four Bhikshus, and the chief King was Buddha himself.]

[1] He is called "uddhamsotas" (qui sublime fertur) F.

SECTION XXV.

ANGER (KODHAVAGGO).

1. In days of old, when Buddha was residing in the Gridhrakûta Mount, near Râjagriha, then Devadatta, in concert with Ajâtaśatru Râja, contrived a plan for the destruction of the Teacher and his followers. The plan was this:—That the King should prohibit the people of the town from giving anything in charity to the community, and so, when they had found their begging excursion through the streets ineffective, that then the King should ask them all to an entertainment at the palace. Meantime Devadatta, having intoxicated 500 elephants, was to let them loose on the Teacher and his followers, and so destroy them all. Accordingly, the invitation was given and accepted by Buddha, and so on the morrow they entered the city as agreed upon. On this the elephants, having been let loose, with upraised trunks, came bellowing down on the crowd, on which the 500 Rahats who followed Buddha rose into the air (and flew away), but Buddha, with Ânanda by his side, checked the fury of the beasts, who now came and bowed down, and went before the Teacher perfectly subdued. On this Buddha, raising the five fingers of his hand, caused the appearance of five lions, who uttered their roar, whilst the earth shook, and the elephants lay down affrighted on the ground. Hereupon Buddha and his followers proceeded to the King's palace, and after listening to the confession of the King, Buddha uttered these stanzas:—

"Amongst men there is no one who is not blamed, from old time till now.[1] Since they blame the man of many words, they blame the patient and quiet man; they also blame the man who seeks the happy medium; there is always blame in the world. Those who desire to find fault with the righteous (holy) man are never able to discriminate with impartiality (take a middle course); they blame him entirely or they praise him entirely, but it is all done from some false idea of profit or fame.[2] But he whom the enlightened and wise praise, and whom they consider and call upright and good, a man of true wisdom and innocent life, without any ground for censure in himself, as a Rahat for purity, there is no blame for him—such an one the gods themselves must admire, even Brahma and Śakra must praise such an one."

Having concluded these stanzas, the World-honoured One related this anecdote:—"There was in days gone by a certain King, who loved above all things the flesh of the wild goose for his daily food. Consequently he used to keep a hunter (or fowler) for the express purpose of snaring these birds, and providing flesh for the royal table. One day the fowler having gone out for this purpose, there came a flock of geese, 500 in number, with their king at their head, and alighted in search of food just where the snares were set. In consequence the king of the birds was trapped, and remained entangled in the toils. Then the rest, in consternation, flew round and round the place, but would not leave it. One of the geese in particular kept flying close by the net, and, undaunted by the arrows of the fowler, kept uttering piteous cries,

[1] Compare ver. 227 of the Pâli.

[2] These verses are very obscure.

whilst the drops of blood (from her wounds) kept falling on the ground, and so from morn till eve she continued to act. Then the fowler, moved with compassion, liberated the king of the birds, and joyfully he flew away to rejoin the flock. On relating this to the King, he highly approved of what he had done in liberating the bird. Now at that time, Buddha said, I was the king of the wild geese, Ânanda was the faithful bird that would not leave me, you, O King! were the King of the country, and the huntsman was Devadatta, who has ever sought to do me harm (but on this occasion I do not withhold from him some portion of praise for his humane conduct) [such at least appears to be the moral of the story]."

SECTION XXVI.

IMPURITY (MALAVAGGO).

1. THERE was once a man who had no brothers, but only one little son, who was much beloved by both his parents. They procured for him means of instruction, and fondly hoped that he would be an honour to their house. But, alas! he was careless and negligent, and learned nothing. In consequence of this his parents took him to their home, and hoped he would be useful in the management of the house. But he was idle and dirty in his ways, and altogether a grief to them. In consequence of this he was slighted by all the neighbours, and became an object of contempt amongst his friends, and almost hateful to his parents. Deeply touched by this, he sought some comfort in religious exercises, but found no help in all his penances and prayers to the gods. At last, hearing that Buddha was the all-wise Teacher who could meet the necessities of his case, he came to him and begged his help. To whom Buddha replied, "If you would find comfort in my society, the first thing for you to learn is purity of conduct. Go back, therefore, to your home, and learn to obey your parents, recite your prayers, be diligent in your daily occupations, let no love of ease tempt you to neglect cleanliness of person or decency of dress; and then, having learned this, come back to me, and you may perhaps be allowed to enter into the companionship of my followers." And then the World-honoured added these stanzas:—

"Absence[1] of (daily) prayer is the disease of

[1] Compare ver. 241 of the Pâli.

(daily) conversation (words). Want of diligence is the disease of a household. Want of becoming dignity is the disease of manner (outward appearance). Carelessness is the disease of business. Stinginess is the disease of charity. Vice is the disease of daily conduct. Both now and hereafter an evil Rule of life (Law) is an everlasting disease (taint). But the disease of all diseases, than which none is worse, is ignorance.[1] He who is wise (enlightened) should free himself from this. Then, O Bhikshus! there is no disease."

The man having heard these words, and perceiving that ignorance (in the sense of "folly," or "infatuation") was at the bottom of all his misfortunes, returned to his father's house, and gave himself up to obey and to work; he paid respect to his teacher, and was constant in the recitation of the Scriptures, and in all respects ordered his life diligently and circumspectly, and after three years returned to Buddha, and having paid homage to him, related how he had changed his life, and now besought admission into his society. On this the World-honoured One addressed him in these words, "Welcome, O youth!" and at once, his hair falling off, he became a Shaman, and by an inward effort of mind arrived at a knowledge of the four truths, and became after a day's perseverance a complete Rahat.

[1] *Moha, i.e.*, delusion; not *avidyâ*. The Pâli text gives *avijjâ*, however.

SECTION XXVII.

FIRMLY HOLDING BY THE LAW (DHAMMATTHVAGGO).

1. THERE was once a very old Brahman, called Sa-che (Sacha or Satya) Nirgrantha, celebrated for his acuteness in discussion. He had 500 disciples, and all of them were so self-opinionated with regard to their superior learning that they used to clothe themselves with iron plates, lest their wisdom should overflow and run to waste (*sic.*). Now when Sacha heard that Buddha had come into the world, and was converting men by his superior wisdom, he was filled with jealousy, and could not rest at night from very envy, and therefore, addressing his disciples, he said, "I hear that the Shaman Gotama professes to be a Buddha. I will go and ask him a few questions, and make him blush for shame when he finds he cannot answer them." Accordingly, he with his followers went to the Jetavana (Vihâra), and as they stood without seeing the glory of Buddha's person, like the sun when he first comes forth in his strength, they were overpowered and confused by their feelings, and so passing through the door they came before Buddha, and did him reverence. On this Buddha requested them to be seated. Being so seated, the Nirgrantha asked Buddha as follows:—"Who is the just man? Who is the learned man? Who is the reverend man? What is true beauty and grace?[1] What is a Shaman? Who is a true Bhikshu? and who is the truly enlightened? and who the obedient man (who respectfully observes the rules of moral

[1] Or, Who is the upright man? (*twan ching*).

conduct)? If you are able, be pleased to answer these questions for the sake of my followers."

On this the World-honoured, perceiving exactly how the case lay, answered in these stanzas :—

"The man who is always anxious and desirous to learn, who walks uprightly, who ponders on and considers the character of precious wisdom, this man is called Just (*i.e.*, Righteous; one who has attained the way, or Bôdhi). And who is the man of Knowledge? He who depends not on any fine distinction of words—who is free from fear and from apprehension, who stands by what is right—he is the man of Knowledge. And who is the Reverend man (aged)? Not he who has come to old age (sexegenarian)—his form bent, his hair white—for with all that he may be but a fool. But he who ponders on and inquires into the Law (the Dharma), who regulates and restrains his conduct, (is full of) love and virtue, who is able to penetrate into hidden secrets, and is pure—this man is rightly called 'Reverend.' And who is the graceful and perfect man? Not he who possesses beauty of form like the flowers (that charm us); not he who covets and longs for the empty vanities of personal adornment; not he whose words and conduct are opposed to one another; but he who is able to give up every vicious way, who has got rid of it from the very root, who is enlightened without a remnant of hatred—this man is truly graceful and upright (or respectable, *i.e.*, admirable in conduct).[1]

[1] The phrase *twan ching* properly means "upright in conduct."

And who is the Shaman? Not he who is shaven perforce, who speaks untruth, and covets possession, or who is a slave of desire like the rest of men; but he who is able to put an end to (to compose) every wicked (desire), to silence every personal preference, to quiet his mind, and put an end to thought—this man is called a Shaman. And who is called a Bhikshu? Not he who at stated times begs his food; not he who walks unrighteously (heretically), but hopes to be considered a disciple, desiring to establish a character (as a religious person), and that is all; but he who gives up every cause (karma) of guilt, and who lives continently and purely, who by wisdom is able to crush every evil (inclination)—this man is a true Bhikshu. And who is the truly enlightened (or the wise man)? Not he who is simply mute, whilst the busy work of his mind is impure—merely accommodating himself to the outer rule and that is all; but he whose heart is without preference (indifferent), whose inward life is pure and spiritual (empty), perfectly unmoved and dead to this or that (person or thing)—this man is called an inwardly enlightened man (Muni?) And who is a man of Bôdhi (an Ariya or 'elected one')? Not he who saves the life of all things, but he who is filled with universal benevolence, who has no malice in his heart—he is a man of Bôdhi. And the man who observes the Law is not he who talks much, but one who keeps his body (himself) in subjection to the Law (Religion), although he be a plain, untaught man, always guarding the way (of truth) without any forgetfulness—this man is an observer of the Law[1] (*i.e.*, Dhammaṭṭho)."

On hearing these words, Sacha Nirgrantha and his 500 followers were all filled with joy, and became followers of Buddha (Shamans). The Nirgrantha arrived at the condition (heart) of a Bôdhisatwa, the others became Rahats.

[1] These verses agree generally with the Pâli.

SECTION XXVIII.

THE WAY (MAGGAVAGGO).

1. In days of old there was a Brahman, who when young had left his home for the purpose of religious seclusion, and who remained a solitary student till he was sixty years of age, but even after this long period he was unable to arrive at supreme wisdom (Bôdhi). Now, according to the law of the Brahmans, if a man at sixty years of age has not reached wisdom, it is his duty to return to his home and marry a wife. Accordingly, the man having so done, there was born to him a very graceful boy, who when seven years of age, being already deeply read in the books of his religion, and possessed of wonderful dialectic skill, was suddenly struck by a fatal disease and died. The father, overwhelmed by sorrow, gave himself up to immoderate grief, and was quite unable to control himself. He threw himself on the corpse of his child, and lay there as one dead. On recovering himself, the child's body was enshrouded and coffined—the father having been remonstrated with by his relatives and those of his caste—and finally taken without the city for interment. On this occasion the Brahman began to reflect with himself thus—"What use is it thus giving way to tears? It is not of any service; but I will go at once to the abode of Chen-lo-wang (Yamarâja), and beg him humbly to give me back my child alive." On this the Brahman, having gone through certain religious rites and offered flowers and incense, departed from his home, and wherever he came he asked of all he met whether they knew where Yamarâja

held his court and ruled. After wandering onwards thus for several thousand lis, he came to a deep mountain pass, where he met with a party of Brahmans who had acquired supreme wisdom. He inquired again of these if they could tell him where Yamarâja ruled and held his court. To this they replied, "And why do you, honourable sir, desire to know?" On this he told them his sad grief, and explained his intention to beg back his child from the God of the lower world. Then all the Brahmans, pitying his self-delusion, replied—"No mortal man can reach the place where Yama reigns; but about 400 lis to the westward of this place there is a great valley, in the midst of which there is a city. In this city the gods and heavenly spirits, who sometimes dwell among men, take up their abode, and Yama, on the eighth day of the month, constantly visits the spot. By going there, and practising a strictly religious mode of life, you may, honourable sir, see the King of the Dead." Then the Brahman, rejoiced to hear this news, departed, and arriving at this valley, lo! in the midst of it he saw a beautiful city with palaces, and towers, and residences, like those in the Trâyastriñshas Heaven. Then coming before the gate, he began to burn incense, and recite his religious formularies (Mantras), with a view to gain admission and obtain sight of Yamarâja. At length he was admitted into the dread presence of the King, and, on being asked his wish, he related his case as before. To him the King thus replied—"What you ask, honourable sir, is pious and good of you. Your son is now in the Eastern garden disporting himself there; take him and go." On this the Brahman forthwith hastened to the place, and there he saw his loved child playing with other children. He immediately ran to him, and embracing him, with the tears coursing down his cheeks, exclaimed—"How can I forget you, my child, over whom I have watched so long and lovingly! Remember you not me, my child, your father? Do you not recall our grief as we tended you in your sickness, my child?" But the boy repelled the embrace of the Brahman, and upbraided him for using such foolish terms as father and child, who perish as the grass. "In my present state," he added, "I know no such words, and I am free from such delusive thoughts." On this the Brahman, with many tears, departed; and as he went he bethought himself of the Shaman Gôtama, and he resolved to go to him and lay bare his grief, and seek for some consolation. Accordingly he arrived at the Jetavana, and having paid the usual homage, he explained his circumstances, and how his child had refused to come back with him. To him replied the World-honoured—"Truly you are self-deluded and foolish, for when the spirit of a dead man departs, know you not that it forthwith receives another bodily form, and then all the relative terms of father, son, wife, mother, are at an end, just as a guest who leaves his lodging has done with it as though it were a thing of the past? Sad is your case, and much to be pitied, not to know that such changes will ever go on till you reach a condition of true wisdom, and give up, once for all, every thought about such worldly things as these. In this way alone can you make an end of future birth and death, and become for ever free." And then he added these stanzas:—

"Men concern themselves about the matters of wife and child; they perceive not the inevitable law of disease (and death), and the end of life which quickly comes, as a bursting torrent (sweeping all before it) in a moment.[1] Then neither father or mother can save one; what hope, then, can be placed in all one's relatives (kinsfolk)? At the end of life parent and kinsman are as a blind man set to look after (keep) a burning lamp. A wise man understanding this should carefully practise himself in

[1] Compare ver. 287 of the Pâli.

the Rules of Religion (moral life); he should walk diligently so as to help (save) the world, with a view to destroy completely (the sources of) sorrow, to get away from the seething whirlpool (of life and death); as the wind drives away the clouds, so should he strive to destroy all remnant of thought (consciousness, 'sañjña);' this is the office of knowledge. Wisdom is superior to all worldly (devices) —it makes a man indifferent to its joys, and renders him unconcerned about its business; whoever receives this true instruction shall get rid for ever of renewed birth and death."

On hearing these verses the Brahman at once obtained enlightenment and perceived the inconstancy of life; that wife and child are but as the guest who leaves the house; and so having paid reverence to Buddha, he besought permission to enter the community, on which Buddha having welcomed him, he at once became a Shaman, and eventually arrived at the condition of a Rahat.

SECTION XXIX.

WIDE AND DIFFUSIVE (SENTENCES).[1]

1. IN days of old when Buddha was residing in the country of Śrâvastî, preaching his doctrine for the conversion of the various orders of creatures (gods, nâgas, men, &c.), it happened that the king of the country, who was called Prasenajita, had gone on three occasions with his ministers to hear Buddha's discourses. Now at this time the king had given way to much self-indulgence in the way of luxurious living and other gratifications of the senses, in consequence of which he had become sleek and fat, and being so, he suffered from various ailments, such as flatulency and excessive drowsiness and heaviness, so that he could scarcely rise up without inconvenience, and was always more or less a sufferer from discomfort.

In this condition he once came to the place where Buddha was, and leaning on the arms of his attendants, he took his seat, and with clasped hands addressed the teacher thus:—"World-honoured! pardon, I pray, my want of due respect in not saluting you as I ought, but I know not what ailment possesses me that I am become so fat! and it is this that pains me so that I can pay none of the usual respects to your person." To which the Lord replied—"Mahârâja! there are five things which always produce the condition of which you complain: 1st, constantly eating; 2d, love of sleep; 3d, love of pleasure; 4th, absence of thought; 5th, want of occupation. These are the things that cause corpulency

[1] Translated "Miscellaneous" from the Pâli *pakinnako*.

and grossness of habit; if you would escape from this condition, then you must give up your luxurious living, and afterwards you will become thin again. And then the Lord added these stanzas:—

"A man ought to recollect and consider at every meal to exercise self-control, and thus avoid those aches and pains to which we are constantly liable; by allowing time for taking food, he causes his life to be prolonged."

On hearing these verses, the king was so gratified that he ordered his chief cook to remember them, and to recite them in his presence before and after every meal. By doing thus the king was able to restrain himself, and gradually recovered his lightness of body and animal spirits, at which he was so rejoiced, that one day he went afoot to the place where Buddha was, and coming into his presence he paid him homage. On the Lord requesting him to be seated, he inquired, "Where, O king, are your horses and chariot, how is it that you have come here afoot?" On which the king answered with joy—"By attending to what Buddha on a former occasion taught me, I have become light of body again, so that I find no difficulty whatever in walking as I have to the place where we are now assembled." Then Buddha addressed the king as follows:—"Mahârâja! it is because men do not consider the impermanence of things in the world that matters are as they are. They nourish and cherish their bodies and their appetites, not remembering even their own comfort (happiness) in so doing, and thus the man dies and his spirit departs, whilst his body decays in the tomb. The wise man nourishes his soul (spirit), the foolish man nourishes his body. If you can understand this, then you may prepare yourself to receive the sacred teaching (of my doctrine)," and then the Lord added these verses:—

"How impermanent is man! he grows old as the stalled ox, fat, and fleshy, and strong, but he has no saving wisdom; without thought of life and death, and the perpetual troubles involved in them, thinking only of the body and its wants, and thus adding to his sorrows without prospect of escape. But the wise man understanding (the cause of) sorrow, on this account lets his body go; he destroys all thought (about it), he cuts off desire, and thus making an end of all lustful appetites, he also puts an end to renewed birth."

The king having heard these words and understood them, at once received enlightenment, and others who heard them in great numbers, arrived at the "eyes of the law" (religious illumination).

2. In days of old there were seven mendicants, who together resorted to the mountain wilds for the purpose of acquiring supreme wisdom. After twelve years' fruitless effort, they began to reason amongst themselves and say: "To acquire supreme wisdom is very hard; to mortify one's body and cramp one's limbs, and to endure cold and pain without interval, and to beg one's food and receive such scant supplies, all this is hard. To persevere in the path (of duty) so as to avoid any fault (sin) is hard. Why then do we any longer consume away our life in the mountain wilds? Surely this course is not so agreeable as to return home and establish our families, and marry wives and have children, and enjoy ourselves to the end of our days." On this the seven men agreed to leave the mountains, and so went on their way homeward.

Now Buddha, knowing their case, and perceiving there was a possibility of their salvation, out of pity to them, knowing that their impatience in religious exercises would, if allowed to go on, end in their ruin, transformed himself into the appearance of a Shaman, and transporting himself to the midst of a narrow defile, met them as they came along. And then he asked them, "After so long a trial in searching for supreme wisdom, why are ye leaving (the mountains, and giving up the quest)?" To which they replied, "To gain wisdom (*i.e.*, complete illumination, or Bôdhi) is difficult. To attend diligently (in extirpating) the root of sorrow and sin is difficult. To go a-begging through the town, and receive scant charity, is hard. And to live here in the mountains, with no one to nourish us, in constant discomfort to the end of one's days, this is unbearable; and we are therefore going home to engage in our worldly occupations and get wealth, and then when we are old we will give ourselves up to seek for supreme wisdom."

The Shaman replied, "Stand still awhile, and listen to me. 'Man's life is inconstant; a morning and an evening, and it may be gone. Although the way of religion is hard, yet it is but the sorrow first which leads to the joy which follows. To live in the world[1] is also hard; through endless ages to have the cares of wife and child, without interval of rest. To live in community, and to take the vows of equality in all earthly goods, looking forward to and anticipating future happiness without interval of sorrow, this is difficult. The present life is but a scene of constant struggle against disease and hurts; wherever there is bodily existence, there is pain and sorrow. He only who has faith, and lives religiously (observing the moral rules), his heart intent on gaining supreme wisdom, with no interval of carelessness or remission of duty, to him alone there is an end, an eternal end, of misery." On this the Shaman resumed the glorious appearance of Buddha, and spake these stanzas:—

"To aim at supreme wisdom and to give up sin is hard; but to live in the world as a worldly

[1] That is, *a secular life.*

man is also hard.[1] To dwell in a religious community on terms of perfect equality as to worldly goods is difficult; but difficult beyond comparison is the possession of worldly goods (or, 'it is difficult not to transgress in having such goods'). To beg one's food as a mendicant is hard, but what can a man do who does not restrain himself? By perseverance the duty becomes natural, and in the end there is no desire to have it otherwise. Having faith, then duty is easily accomplished; from following in the path of duty (*i.e.*, moral duty) a man greatly enriches himself, and from this, moreover, it results that wherever he is, by whomsoever seen, he is respected (cherished). Sitting alone, occupying one place for sleep, ceaselessly pursuing one line of conduct (walk, or action), jealously guarding one upright (or correct) state of mind, there will be of necessity joy to such a man (though) living in the forest."

On hearing these words the seven mendicants, filled with shame on account of their behaviour, bowed themselves down at the Lord's feet, and returning to the mountain wilds, and continuing to guard "one perfect heart," they attained supreme wisdom, and became Rahats.

[1] There is a general agreement here with ver. 302 of the Pâli.

SECTION XXX.

HELL (NIRAYAVAGGO).

1. In olden time there was in the country of Śrâvastî a certain Brahman teacher called Purâna Kâśyapa (Pou-lan-ka-ye), who had five hundred followers, who went about the country with their master, and were greatly respected by the King and people. Now it came to pass that after Buddha had attained supreme wisdom, and when with his disciples he had come to Śrâvastî, that, on account of his personal dignity, and the character of his teaching, the King and people paid him great respect. On this Kâśyapa was full of jealousy, and he determined to destroy (overthrow) the World-honoured in argument, and cause his death. Accordingly he went, accompanied by his followers, to meet the King, and having found him, he spake thus: "In former days, Mahârâja, you and the people used to attend to me as a teacher, and supply my wants; but since this Sramana Gôtama has arrived here, who falsely says he has become enlightened (Buddha), you have left me, to attend on him. I desire, therefore, that you would allow a discussion between us, and whoever is defeated in argument let him be put to death." The King being pleased with the proposition, submitted it to the World-honoured One, who consented to meet Kâśyapa, as he wished, at the expiration of seven days. Accordingly the King prepared a place standing eastward of the city, smooth and wide, on which he erected two lofty thrones, and adorned them with all sorts of flags and decorations. On these the two disputants were to sit,

with their adherents beneath, and the King and his court between the two. The day having come, Kâśyapa and his followers arrived first, and having ascended his throne, lo! an evil spirit, knowing the envy that burned in the heart of the Brahman, caused a sudden storm to arise, which blew down the seat which he occupied, and filled the whole arena with dust and flying sand. But now Buddha arrived, and having taken his place, the King came forward and entreated him by his power to convert the people to his doctrine, and confute the heretical views of his opponent. On this the Lord ascended into the air, and exhibited his glory in causing fire and water to proceed from his body; and after various miraculous changes in his appearance, he returned once more to his seat. Then the Nâgas and spirits of the air caused flowers and pleasant perfumes to fall, whilst melodious chants were heard in the sky, and the earth and heavens were shaken. Then Purâṇa Kâśyapa, knowing that he had no real claim to the character of a supreme teacher, hung down his head in shame, and dared not lift up his eyes. On this a diamond-Litchavi (hero of Vaiśâlî), raising his mace, from the head of which proceeded sparks of fire, over Kâśyapa, asked him why he did not also display such wonderful changes as those just witnessed? Whereupon Kâśyapa and his followers fled in every direction, and Buddha and his disciples returned to the Jetavana Vihâra, in Śrâvastî. After this Kâśyapa, having met an old female disciple, who ridiculed him for attempting to dispute with Buddha, he came to the banks of the river, and told his disciples that he was now going to ascend to the heaven of Brahmâ, and if after casting himself into the river he did not return, that they might know he had ascended to that heaven. Accordingly he threw himself in, and not returning, his disciples concluded he had gone to heaven; and they also, desiring to join him there, threw themselves one by one into the river, and were lost—going to hell. Then Buddha explained that the two great crimes of Kâśyapa which led to his destruction were these—1st, pretending falsely to have arrived at supreme wisdom; 2d, having wickedly slandered Buddha. And for these two sins he and his followers have gone to perdition; and then he repeated these stanzas:—

"He who, by false assumptions, seeks reward; he who, having done a thing, has not in so doing acted uprightly; he who has maliciously slandered an innocent man, and would control the world by (such) false pretences—that man, dragged down by his guilt, must fall into hell; as a man confined in a stronghold outside a city, guarded without and within, cannot escape, such is his lot. Carefully guarding one's heart, no unholy thought can arise; but failing in this, misery accrues, and in the end that man goes to perdition."

On this Buddha relates an anecdote of five hundred monkeys with their king, who had quarrelled with another king and his followers, and who, being unable to sustain the conflict, ended their lives as Kâśyapa and his followers had done (*i.e.*, by jumping into the sea in search of a beautiful mountain full of delicious fruits, &c., and on the king not returning, his attendants all followed his example, and perished). These five hundred monkeys, Buddha explained, were Kâśyapa and his followers.

The King having heard these words, was filled with joy, and departed.

SECTION XXXI.

THE ELEPHANT (NÁGAVAGGO).

1. In days of old, before Rahula had attained to supreme wisdom, his natural disposition being somewhat low and disorderly, his words were not always marked by love of truth. On one occasion Buddha had ordered him to go to the Kien-tai (Ghanda or Ghanta?) Vihâra, and there remain guarding his mouth (tongue), and governing his thoughts, at the same time diligently studying (or observing) the rules of conduct laid down in the Scriptures. Rahula, having heard the command, made his obeisance and went. For ninety days he remained in deep shame and penitence. At length Buddha repaired to the place, and showed himself; on seeing him, Rahula was filled with joy, and reverently bowed down and worshipped him. After this, Buddha having taken the seat provided for him, he desired Rahula to fill a water-basin with water and bring it to him, and wash his feet. Having done so, and the washing being over, Buddha asked Rahula if the water so used was now fit for any purpose of domestic use (drinking, &c.); and on Rahula replying in the negative, because the water was defiled with dust and dirt, Buddha added: "And such is your case, for although you are my son, and the grandchild of the King, although you have voluntarily given up everything to become a Shaman, nevertheless you are unable to guard your tongue from untruth and the defilement of loose conversation, and so you are like this defiled water—useful for no further pur-

pose." And again he asked him, after the water had been thrown away, whether the vessel was now fit for holding water for drink; to which Rahula replied, "No," for the vessel is still defiled, and is known as an unclean thing, and therefore not used for any purpose such as that indicated; to which Buddha again replied, "And such is your case, by not guarding your tongue, &c., you are known and recognised as unfit for any high purpose, although you profess to be a Shaman." And then once more lifting the empty basin on to his foot, and whirling it round and round, he asked Rahula if he were not afraid lest it should fall and be broken; to which Rahula replied that he had no such fear, for the vessel was but a cheap and common one, and therefore its loss would be a matter of small moment. "And such is your case," again said Buddha, "for though you are a Shaman, yet being unable to guard your mouth or your tongue, you are destined, as a small and insignificant thing, to be whirled in the endless eddies of transmigration—an object of contempt to all the Wise." Rahula being filled with shame, Buddha addressed him once more: "Listen, and I will speak to you in a parable. There was in old time the king of a certain country who had a large and very powerful elephant, able to overpower by its own strength five hundred smaller elephants. This king, being about to go to war with some rebellious dependency, brought forth the iron armour belonging to the elephant, and directed the master of the animal to put it on him, to wit, two sharp-pointed swords on his tusks, two iron hooks (scythes) on his ears, a crooked spear on each foot, an iron club (or ball) attached to his tail; and to accompany him were appointed nine soldiers as escort. Then the elephant-master was rejoiced to see the creature thus equipped, and trained him above all things to keep his trunk well coiled up, knowing that an arrow piercing *that* in the midst must be fatal. But lo! in the middle of the battle the elephant, uncoiling his trunk, sought to seize a sword with it.

On which the master was affrighted, and, in consultation with the king and his ministers, it was agreed that he should no more be brought into the battle-field." In continuation, Buddha said: "Rahula! if men committing the nine faults only guard their tongue as this elephant was trained to guard his trunk, all would be well. Let them guard against the arrow that strikes in the middle! let them keep their mouth, lest they die, and fall into the misery of future births in the three evil paths!" And then he added these stanzas:—

"I am like the fighting elephant, without any fear of the middle arrow (the arrow wounding the middle part). By sincerity and truth I escape the unprincipled man (lawless man). Like the elephant, well subdued and quiet, permits the king to mount on his trunk (offers his trunk for the king to ascend), thus tamed is the reverend man, he also endures truthfully and in faith."

Rahula, hearing these words, was filled with sorrow for his careless disregard of his words, and gave himself up to renewed exertion, and so became a Rahat.

2. In days of old, when Buddha was residing in the Jetavana of Śrâvastî, preaching his doctrine for the sake of angels and men, at this time there was a certain nobleman, a householder (grihapati), named Atidharma (ho-ti-wan), who, having come to the place where Buddha was, after the customary homage, stood on one side and said: "World-honoured! whenever I undertake any religious duty, such as making an offering or other service, I feel harassed and oppressed by some selfish feeling or other, that destroys my peace of mind. Would that of your great love you would explain this." Then the Lord bade him sit down, and forthwith asked him his name, and whence he came. On this, again prostrating himself, he

told his name, and said that in the time of the former king he had been an elephant-tamer. Buddha then asked him what were the rules for elephant-taming, and what the instruments employed? On this he replied, "There are three things we use in this work—1st, an iron-hooked instrument, for holding the mouth and subduing it; 2d, one for depriving the creature of food, and keeping it low; 3d, a large staff, for the purpose of beating it. By these means we gain the mastery over it, and subdue it." Again Buddha asked, "And of these three things, which is the most useful (or important)?" to which he replied, "The hooked-iron that holds the mouth; this is the most effective, for by means of this discipline the creature is tamed so as to permit the King to mount on its back, and is guided and directed without difficulty in battle." Again Buddha asked, "if this was the generally accepted method of taming elephants, and if there was any other?" and on the elephant-tamer replying in the negative, Buddha added, "As you tame the elephant, so you may tame yourself;" and on his inquiring further as to the meaning of this, Buddha continued: "O elephant-tamer! I have also three things by which I subdue all men, and by which each man may subdue himself, and so arrive at the highest condition of unselfishness (*wou-wei*). And what are these three? 1st, by self-control over the tongue, leading one always to observe the truth; 2d, by love, to persuade the hard and obstinate; 3d, by wisdom, to destroy the influence of ignorance and doubt. By these three I subdue all men, and enable them to escape the path of ruin, and to arrive at a condition free from sorrow and any entanglement of renewed birth and death—perfectly unselfish and indifferent (*wou-wei*)." And then the World-honoured added these lines:—

Like the elephant which is called "U-ts'ai" (Dhammapâlaka?)[1] is difficult to hold and to tame,

[1] Compare ver. 324 of the Pâli.

and when bound does not eat a morsel, and only longs to be free; so this mind of mine, in its natural state, went wandering at large, and ever seeking a resting-place, but now I have subdued it, and I can hold it, as the master with the hook holds the elephant. To be glad in the possession of Reason (Bôdhi), and not to let it escape, to be able at any time to hold in and control the mind, this is to be saved from bodily suffering, as the elephant escapes from the ditch into which he has fallen."

The Grihapati, on hearing these words, was led to serious reflection, and eventually attained to a condition of enlightenment, whilst countless others were converted to the truth.

SECTION XXXII.

LUST (TANHÁVAGGO).

1. In days of old when Buddha was residing in the Gridhrakûta mountain, near Râjagriha, preaching the inestimable doctrine for the sake of angels and men, there was a certain man who, having made up his mind to leave his family and become a recluse, came to the place where Buddha was, and desired permission to enter the community (church). On this Buddha required him (after he had permitted him to become a disciple) to go sit beneath a tree in the solitude, and give himself up to meditation. On this the Shaman departed into the mountain wild, more than a hundred *lis* from the Vihâra, and there gave himself up to a solitary life. After three years of self-denial, his heart being still unsubdued, he desired to give up his profession and to return to his home again, saying thus to himself, "This life of asceticism is troublesome and painful, and not to be compared with the happiness derived from domestic society. I will, therefore, return to my wife and family and enjoy myself." On this he made as though he would leave the mountain and return home. Then Buddha, by his omniscience, seeing the condition of this disciple, and knowing that he had a capacity for salvation, transformed himself into the form of a Shaman, and went to meet him on the way. On encountering one another, the transformed Shaman addressed the other and asked whence he came and whether he was going. On this they agreed mutually to rest awhile and sit down together on a convenient spot (level ground)

Seated thus, the disappointed Shaman explained to the other his condition, and confessed that he was going back home from a feeling of failure in his religious exercises. Now it happened while he was speaking, that an old monkey leaving the tree in which he lived, came down into the open and disported himself; then the assumed Shaman asked the other, why was this; to which the last replied: "I have often observed this same monkey come down and behave himself thus, and the reasons for his so doing are two,—1st, he is rejoiced to be free from the care of providing for his wife and his belongings; and 2dly, he is worn and hurt by constantly climbing the tree in which his family live, and so is glad to escape the labour of so doing: for these two reasons he leaves the tree and enjoys himself in the open ground. But meanwhile, as the two were conversing, the monkey retreated from the open space, and re-climbed the tree, on which the strange Shaman addressed the other, and asked if he perceived this, and how he explained it. On which the latter said that it was in consequence of fear and uncertainty that the monkey had gone back to his home; on which the other rejoined: "Such is the case with yourself; it was the anxieties caused by your wife and family that first induced you to find release in these mountain wilds, but now owing to doubt and uncertainty, you are going back to the world, and by so doing you expose yourself to all the evil consequences of renewed birth and consequent death. Whereupon he added these verses:

"As [1] a tree, as long as its root is firm and safe, although cut down, still survives and produces fruit; so, unless the remnants of lust are destroyed and uprooted, (a man) must return again and again to receive sorrow. The monkey, away from the

[1] Compare ver. 338 of the Pâli.

tree, first of all enjoys release, and then returns again (to its bondage), such is the case with men, they escape from hell and then return to it. Longing thoughts are like the ever-flowing waters of a river; giving way to the free enjoyment of indolence and luxury, the mind like a savage dog seeks for continual indulgence, and the man himself becomes clouded and unable to see the truth. Every thought flowing in the same channel, then lusts bind a man as with strong rattan bonds. The wise man alone is able rightly to distinguish the truth, he is able to cut off the very root and source of his (lustful) thoughts. A man by self-indulgence becomes sleek and shining, his thoughts increase like the sprouting tendril, the depth of lust cannot be fathomed; from this proceeds the ever-increasing succession of old age and continual death."

The Bhikshu beholding the glorious appearance of Buddha, and hearing the words of the verses he had uttered, prostrated himself on the earth in lowest reverence before him, and repenting of his sloth, he assiduously practised the rules of Samatha and Vipassinà,[1] arrived at the condition of a Rahat. And all the Devas who had heard the words, with joyful thoughts scattered flowers before the person of Buddha, as a religious offering, and with countless[2] "Sâdhus" departed.

2. In days of old when Buddha was residing at Śrâvastî, and there preaching his doctrine for the good of Devas and men, there was residing in the city a certain rich Brahman of a very covetous and niggard disposition, who, from

[1] For the meaning of these terms (tranquillity and contemplation, the *chi kwan* of the Tien-tai school of Buddhists in China), *vide* Childer's Dict., *sub. voc.*

[2] "Sâdhu"—an expression of approval, as our "Amen."

a desire to save alms, used to order his servant to shut his door and fasten his windows whenever he took his meals, so that no beggar should molest him with his importunities. And so no religious person (Shaman) could ever gain admittance, or stand in the presence of this Brahman. One day having desired his wife to kill a fowl and make a highly savoury dish of the same, they both sat down together to eat it, the doors and the windows having first been closed—and between them their little child, into whose mouth they both occasionally put scraps of the savoury dish. Now Buddha, knowing that there was a capacity for conversion in this man's case, transformed himself into the appearance of a Shaman, and waiting till the master of the house had finished his meal he placed himself before his chair, or seat, and recited the usual formula. "He who gives little or much (or he who gives a little of his abundance) in charity, lays up for himself a great reward." The Brahman, raising his head and seeing the Shaman (as it seemed), began to abuse him and said, "You call yourself a religious mendicant, do you? and yet have no better manners than this, to force yourself into my presence when at my meals with my family?" To which he replied, "It is you, my lord, who ought to be ashamed—I need not feel shame for begging as a mendicant." The Brahman then replied—"And what shame should I feel for eating thus with my wife in comfort?" "You, my lord, who have killed your father, and married your mother, and thus involved yourself in family disgrace, and feel no shame, nevertheless upbraid me and would put me to shame for begging a little food," and then he recited the following verses:—

"As the sprouting creeper which is not cut off (at the root), such is the case of the man who, with covetous desire, partakes of food; ever cherishing evil thoughts and multiplying family discords (tombs), such is the constant employment of the ingorant man. Hell, indeed, has its gyves and fetters, but the wise man regards not these as captivity; the foolish man who is immersed in cares about wife and child and their personal adornment, he it is who is in real captivity. The wise man regards lust as the imprisonment of hell, as the hard bound fetter from which it is difficult to escape, and therefore he desires to separate this and cut it off for ever, that being free from any such cares (or, desires), he may find rest and peace."[1]

The Brahman on hearing these words inquired as to their meaning, on which the Shaman explained, that in former years the bird (cock) which he had just eaten was his father, that the little boy his son had been a Raksha, and had eaten the father, and that his wife had been in former days his mother—and thus it was he was involved in the utmost disgrace. On hearing these words the Brahman, filled with fear, besought Buddha, who had now assumed his glorious appearance, to instruct him in the rules of his society, and finally obtained release and entered the first path.

3. In days of old when Buddha was residing at the Jetavana Vihâra near Śrâvastî, there was a young Bhikshu, who, in going through the streets of the city on a begging excursion, cast eyes on a girl of exceeding beauty, and was filled with passion for her. Being unable to conquer his desire, he fell sick, and was unable to eat or sleep, and pined away daily. On this a fellow disciple went to him, and asked him how it was he suffered thus, on which the first revealed the whole matter to the other, and in the end they both went to the place where Buddha was, and explained the thing to him. On this Buddha promised to find a remedy for the Bhikshu's malady, and forthwith

[1] Compare vers. 345, 346 of the Pâli.

desired him to accompany him with his followers to the city. On going to the house where the maiden had dwelt, they found she had now been dead three days, and the house was filled with mourners, who wailed and wept incessantly. Then pointing to the offensive corpse, Buddha asked the Bhikshu, if it was that which had inflamed him with passion? And he then explained how all things that exist are equally perishable and inconstant, and that only through ignorance of this do men set their hearts upon them, and afterwards he added these verses:—

"At the sight of beauty the heart is at once ensnared, because it considers not the impermanency of all such appearances. The fool regarding the outward form as an excellency, how can he know the falseness of the thing, for like a silkworm[1] enveloped in its own net (cocoon), so is he entangled in his own love of sensual pleasure. But the wise man, able to separate himself and cast off all this, is no longer entangled, but casts away all sorrows. The careless and idle man considers that such indulgence of sense is not contrary to purity, and so going on still indulging such thoughts, he is bound as a captive in hell; but the wise man, destroying all thoughts about such things, and ever remembering the impurity of such indulgence, by this means comes out of captivity, and so is able to escape from the grief of repeated old age and death."

The youthful Bhikshu, seeing the dreadful sight before him, and having heard the verses just recited, turned with

[1] This seems to correspond to the "spider" simile in ver. 347 of the Pâli.

repentance and prostrated himself before Buddha, after which, persevering in the way of purity, he soon became a Rahat.

4. In days of old when Buddha was residing at the Jetavana Vihâra, near Śrâvastî, preaching his law for the sake of Devas and men (Nâgas and demons), there was at this time a certain rich householder who had but one son, a youth of about twelve or thirteen years of age. This boy's father and mother having died, and he not being acquainted with the rules of economising his expenses, began to lavish his money on himself and others, till he soon came to beggary and want. Now the lad's father had a certain relative who also was very rich; this man one day seeing the sad condition of the youth, had compassion on him, and took him to his own house, and finally provided him with an establishment of his own, with a wife, slaves, horses, and chariots. But notwithstanding his former experience, the young man again gave way to extravagance, and was again reduced to poverty, and notwithstanding the repeated help of his kinsman and patron he was ever thus. At length his relative, tired out, sent for the wife of the man, and told her that she had better seek another home, and find some one who could protect and provide for her in a respectable way. On hearing this she returned to her master and said, "My lord, you seem unable to provide for our wants, let me ask you what you intend to do, for it behoves me to seek another home, if there is no provision here for me." On hearing this the man was filled with shame and disappointment, and thought thus with himself—"I am indeed a miserable and unhappy man, not knowing how to manage my affairs; and now I am going to lose my wife, and to be left to beg again." Thinking thus, and excited by recollection of past pleasures and passion, he resolved wickedly to put an end to his wife, and afterwards to kill himself. Taking the woman, therefore, into the inner apartments, he at once told her his intention to die with

her there, and then he stabbed her, and afterwards killed himself. The servants, finding how the case stood, hastily went to the man's rich relation and told him all the circumstances; on this he came with all the people round about, and seeing the sad sight he was filled with grief, and finally buried them according to the fixed rules of the country. Afterwards hearing of Buddha, and the comfort which he was able to give by the preaching of his word, he came with all his attendants to the place where the Master was, and told him of all the things that had befallen him. On this Buddha began the following discourse:—"Lust and passion (angry passion) are the constant miseries of the world. These are the causes of all the unhappiness which befalls the foolish man. These are the means by which the constant repetition of birth in the different conditions of existence (the five ways) is continued throughout the three worlds. If the sufferings of ages cannot bring men to repentance and amendment, how much less can we expect the fool now to become wise, and shake off the poison of this lust and covetous longing, which destroys his body and ruins his family (clan), nay, which destroys and ruins the whole world—and if this be so, how can we wonder at what has befallen this man and his wife. Then the master added these lines:

"The fool self-bound by his covetousness, seeks not to escape to that shore. Coveting wealth and lustful indulgence, he destroys others and he is self-destroyed. The lustful mind is the field, uxoriousness, anger, delusion, are the fruits. Therefore he who bestows charity on the non-worldly man, obtains by so doing boundless happiness (merit). Companions few and goods many,[1] the merchant, timorous and anxious, given to covetous

[1] This is a literal translation—I cannot render it otherwise.

thoughts, the robber takes his life (or, 'these, like a robber, take his life'). The wise man, therefore, puts away all covetous desire."

The householder hearing these words was filled with joy; he forgot his grief, and rising from his seat, he and his associates at once obtained the fruition of the first path.

5. In days of old when Buddha was residing in the Jetavana Vihâra, near Śrâvastî, preaching his word for the sake of Devas and men, &c., there happened to be two wandering fellows who were sworn friends, and as it were one in heart, who being in the neighbourhood thought they would become Shamans. They came accordingly to the place where the master was, and after doing homage they explained their wish. Having admitted them to his community, he sent them to one place to give themselves up to meditation. Notwithstanding all their efforts, however, they were unable to forget the pleasures of their former life, and were enslaved by longing for sensual indulgence. Buddha by his divine sight understanding their condition, and desiring to save them, caused a Shaman to go to their place of abode, and addressing them said, "What think you if we three go to the neighbouring harlot-quarter, and without further ado, have a look at the form of one of the beauties about whom you think so much?" Accordingly they all went to the harlots' quarter, and meeting with one (who was indeed only Buddha himself so transformed), they asked her to let them behold her charms, without actually committing any overt-act of transgression. Accordingly the woman began to take off her wreaths and her jewels, and gradually stripping off her clothes, lo! such a ghastly sight of deformity met their eyes, and such a fetid odour assailed their sense, that they could not come nigh the place where she was. Then the Shaman turned and addressed the two: "What the world calls beauty is but the combination of

flowers and ornaments, unguents and dress; remove these, and what is there but unsightliness and disgusting appearance? Is it with such a form as this, the skin wrinkled like leather, the body exuding foul smells, that you are so madly enamoured, and then he added these verses:

"O lust! I have discovered thy source and origin. Born of the busy recollections that haunt the mind. Now will I no more think of thee or these; then thou shalt not longer exist for me. Of the mind alone is lustful desire; from oneself arise the five longings of sense. Haste, then, to bind these five desires, and prove thyself a hero indeed! Where there is no lust there is no anxious fear; at rest, and quiet, there are no more harrowing cares for such an one—desire expelled, its trammels for ever cast away. This is indeed to find true deliverance (*lit.* "for long to come out of the gulf (of misery))" [probably the same as "Oghatinna," *vide* M.M. 370].

Then Buddha, having assumed his glorious appearance, the two Shamans were filled with shame, and with deep repentance fell down at his feet and did obeisance. And after listening further to his instruction they[1] became Rahats. Now as they were returning to their place of abode, the one seeing the happy, contented face of the other, asked his companion the reason of it, on which he repeated over and over the following lines:—

"Day and night was I a slave of lustful desires, incessantly did my mind dwell on these thoughts; but now I have seen the woman I longed for so

[1] Or, as the following lines would indicate, only one was able to arrive at this condition.

much in all her naked deformity, my thoughts have perished, I have no more sorrow."

On hearing these words, his companion was able to shake off the trammels of lust, and immediately received Divine illumination (eyes of the Law).

SECTION XXXIII.

ADVANTAGEOUS SERVICE.[1]

FORMERLY Buddha with his followers, having gone to the kingdom of Kausâmbî (Ku-tan-mi), he took up his residence in the Vihâra called Mi-yin (lovely sound), and there preached the word for the sake of Devas and men. At this time the king of the country was called Yau-tien (Udâyana), whose queen was of a remarkably pure character. Having heard that Buddha had come to his kingdom, the King and the Queen, with her attendants, went forth to visit him, and having paid him the usual salutations, they sat down. Then Buddha, for their sakes, began to preach and to show the impermanency, sorrow, and vanity of things around us, from which all our miseries come. And then he proved that heaven was the reward of religious merit (virtue), and hell the result of sin (crime). In consequence of this sermon both the King and Queen were induced to accept the five rules of a lay-disciple, and so returned to the palace. Now at this time there was a certain Brahman called Kih-sing (lucky star), who had a daughter incomparable for loveliness, just sixteen years old. On her account the Brahman, for ninety days, exposed a heap of a thousand gold masurans, and challenged any one to find a single fault in her, and whoever could do so should have the gold. No one being able to do so, and desiring to find some one fit for her to marry, he again challenged any one to bring a man equal to his daughter in grace, and to him he would give her as a wife. Now,

[1] This section, as I have already observed, does not occur in the Pâli.

having heard that the family of the Shâman Gôtama, known as the Śâkyas, were remarkable for their beauty, and that therefore he was fit to possess his daughter, he came to the place where Buddha was, and taking his daughter with him, after the usual salutations, he spake thus:—"My daughter is extremely beautiful, and unequalled for womanly grace; and you also, Gôtama, are remarkable for your beauty. You may, therefore, have my daughter, and make her your companion (wife)." To whom Buddha replied, "Your daughter's beauty, sir, is according to your own estimation; my beauty is according to that of the Buddhas; my beauty and a woman's beauty are wholly different. Your daughter's loveliness, O sir, is like that of the picture on the jar (or vessel), in the middle of which there is only filth and excrement. How can that be considered as beauty which belongs only to the eyes, the ears, the nose, the mouth, the body? It is this beauty of outside form that causes sorrow, overturns families, destroys kinship, sacrifices relationships, kills children; all these come from this (love of) womanly beauty. But I am a Shaman—I stand by myself—and would rather endure any calamity than comply with your request. Sir, you may go; I decline your offer."

On this the Brahman departed highly irate; and then, coming into the presence of the King, he dilated on his daughter's beauty, and offered her to him. The King, highly pleased at her appearance, accepted her, and made her his second Queen. Having laden her with presents and jewelry, she soon began to fill his mind with jealous thoughts and dislike for the first Queen, and at last persuaded him to send for her on a certain occasion to indulge her fancy (knowing that she would not come). Consequently the King sent for her, on which the first Queen declined to appear, on the ground that she was engaged in some religious exercise (fast), and so for several occasions. The King, enraged thereat, sent a man with a rope to drag her into his presence; and when she was brought in, he took his bow and purposed to shoot her through the body. But lo! the arrow he discharged returned again towards the King, and did her no harm; and so again and again. On this the King, filled with astonishment (fear), said to her, "By what power of magic have you been able to bring this about?" To which she replied, "I have but taken refuge in the three gems, and the whole day have been engaged in religious observances (fasts), and on this account the Lord (World-honoured) has protected me." On this the King exclaimed, "Wonderful!" and, dismissing the second Queen, he sent her back to her parents, and re-established the first in undisputed authority. Then, with the Queen's attendants, he went to the place where Buddha was, and after due salutations, he explained to him what had happened, on which Buddha (after a short discourse) repeated these lines:—

"If Heaven were to rain down the seven precious substances, yet would not the covetous man be satisfied; his pleasure would be little, his sorrow much. The wise man, possessed of virtue, although he possessed the pleasures of Heaven, would wisely let them go, and covet them not. He who finds his happiness in removing thoughts of lustful enjoyment, this man is the disciple of Buddha."

Then Buddha further explained to the King the inevitable result of a wicked life, that it would redound ten thousand times more miserably on the guilty man, whilst the reward of religion and self-denial would be certainly the enjoyment of heaven. Having so spoken, the King and the Queen's attendants, and the rest, received perfect release, and became partakers in the Paths.

SECTION XXXIV.

THE SHAMAN (BHIKKHUVAGGO).

In days of old, when Buddha was residing in the Jetavana Vihâra, near Śrâvastî, preaching his doctrine for the sake of Devas and men, there was a certain Bhikshu, young in years, who used every morning to assume his robe, and take his mendicant's staff and begging-dish, and go through the streets of the town begging his food. On the way there was a certain nobleman's garden, on the outside part of which were sown certain esculant plants, and the ground guarded by a contrivance for discharging arrows at whatever beast, or thief, came there to trespass or steal. Moreover, as guardian of the ground, there was a girl of tender age left, who used to warn travellers away from the place if they had missed their way, or were likely to trespass on the field without knowing the danger, lest they should be shot.

Now it came to pass that on one occasion the Bhikshu, having gone his round through the city, was returning homewards, when, on passing the spot, he heard the plaintive alarm of the girl as she sang out to him to beware; and his passions being roused thereby, he thought to go in and hold some conversation with her, and amuse himself. While assaying to do this he was filled with sudden fear, he let his staff fall, and his robes were disordered, and his alms-dish disarranged; when Buddha, by his divine sight, seeing how the case stood, and that in a moment or two the Bhikshu would be pierced by the arrows, and so perish in his sin, transformed himself into a white-robed layman, and standing by the side of the Bhikshu, repeated these expostulatory stanzas :—

"O Shaman! whither goest thou? unguarded in the workings of thought. Step by step becoming more immersed in the slough, as you follow your evil purpose. Disgrace not your robes by such evil conduct as you purpose! Death stares you in the face as you go forward! Stem the stream (of inclination), pause and reflect, trample down the lustful desire. A man who does not destroy desire is led on by one thought alone (to do this and that, till he destroys and ruins himself). Be up then, and dare to do! Bind thyself fast. The man who has left home (to become a Shaman), and yet gives way to idleness and sloth—whose mind still hankers after impure indulgence—is like the rotten tree against which the wind blows, which can hardly resist its force, but is soon blown down."

Then Buddha, having assumed his glorious appearance, the Bhikshu, ashamed of his weakness, fell down at the master's feet, and, deeply repenting, soon became a Rahat; and countless others who heard the circumstances, belonging to the Vihâra, received divine illumination.

SECTION XXXV.

THE BRAHMACHÂRIN.

IN days of old, in a certain mountain (called Sse-yau-chu-to) in the country of Saketa (Sse-ho-teh), there were resident some 500 Brahmans who pretended to have arrived at final release (Nirvâna), in consideration of their miraculous powers (irrdhi). Now at this time Buddha, having just arrived at complete enlightenment, and beginning to sound the drum of the law, and open the doors of immortality, was induced, on account of these Brahmachârins, to come into their neighbourhood, and sitting beneath a tree, to reveal the splendour of his person. After some conversation with them, he repeated these verses:

"Stem the stream and pass over, without desire as a Brahman! Understanding the end of all that is made (or, of all modes of conduct), this is truly named (the life of a) Brahmachârin.[1] In (or, by means of) the two laws of nothingness,[2] pure and spotless passing over the gulf, casting off all the bonds of desire, this is to be a Brahmachârin (indeed). It is not by his clan, or his platted hair, that a man is called a Brahman, but he who walks truthfully and righteously, he is indeed rightly called a good man (Bhadra). What avails the

[1] The reader will observe the similarity of the Pâli version, vers. 383, &c.

[2] The sense appears to be "regarding both this world and the other as nothing." Compare the Pali *orapâra*.

platted hair, O fool! the garment of grass, what good? Within there is no quittance of desire, then what advantage the outward denial of self? Put away lust, hatred, delusion, sloth and all its evil consequences, as the snake puts off its skin, this is to be a Brahmachârin indeed. Separate yourself from all worldly associations—let the mouth speak no foul words—thoroughly investigate the eight paths (Ashtânga mârga), this is to be a Brahmachârin indeed. To have cast off all thoughts of family affection, to have given up all desire after home, and all the bonds of personal preference loosed, this is to be a Brahmachârin indeed. He who has given up all thoughts about this world or the next, and places no reliance on either—this man is a Brahmachârin indeed. He who understands his own previous history, and has come to an end of all future chance of birth or death, him I call a Brahmachârin. He who is perfect in knowledge, is a Brahmachârin."

Having thus spoken, Buddha addressed the Brahmachârins in these words:

"You who profess to have arrived at Nirvâna, are but as fishes in a pool of shallow water! What pleasure or satisfaction can you expect?"

The Brahmachârins having heard these words and considered them, bowed down before Buddha, and having been admitted into his community, soon became Rahats. The other hearers, also filled with joy, were enabled to enter the Paths.

SECTION XXXVI.

NIRVÂNA.[1]

In days of old when Buddha was residing in the Gridhrakûta Mountain, near Râjagriha, with the whole assembly of the Bhikshus, 1250 in number, the King of Magadha, whose name was Ajâtaśatru, being then ruler of 100 kingdoms, was in perplexity as to one of them called Yuechi (Getæ ?), which refused to pay him tribute, although the country abounded in wealth, and was highly prosperous. On this the King sent his prime minister called Yu-she, to ask Buddha what he should do, and whether he would be successful in using force against the rebellious kingdom. Having come into the presence of Buddha and put the question, the World-honoured replied: "So long as the King of the Yue-chi observes the seven rules, he will not be easily overcome." On this the minister inquired as to the character of these seven rules, to which the master answered: (1.) "So long as the people of the Yue-chi observe right rules in self-government, in their several villages and communities, so long they will be able to protect themselves. (2.) So long as the ministers and rulers hold together, and agree, and govern justly, so long, &c. (3.) So long as they in a national view, obey the laws, and submit to their direction without partiality or favour, so long they will be unconquerable. (4.) So long as the Yue-chi observe the rules of decorum between man and woman, and depart not from these rules of propriety, so long, &c. (5.) So long as the Yue-chi observe

[1] The chapters which follow are not found in the Pâli.

the rules of reverence due to father and mother and other relations, and dutifully provide for their wants, so long, &c. (6.) So long as the Yue-chi religiously observe the ceremonies of the four seasons, in doing homage to heaven and earth, so long, &c. (7.) So long as the Yue-chi pay respect to all their religious teachers (Shamans), and especially those who have come to them from far (travellers or religious guests), and provide them with the usual necessaries, such as food, bedding, medicine, &c., so long, &c.

These are the seven rules, if the Yue-chi observe only one of them, it would be difficult to overpower them, how much more if they regard the seven, and then the World-honoured added these words:—

"Rely not too entirely on the advantage of victory (conquest), for though you may prevail in battle, yet there is still sorrow in store; rather should a man seek the rules of self-conquest, having conquered himself, then there will be no further ground for birth (or, continued life)."

The minister having heard these words, was immediately convinced (obtained the rudiments of truth (wisdom or Bôdhi)), and those in the assembly who had not yet entered the Paths, were enabled to do so. The minister then rising from his seat, begged permission to depart, and on being so permitted by Buddha, he went back to the King and told him what the master had said. On this the King gave up all his intentions to go to war, and in consequence the Yue-chi returned to their obedience and submitted to the King.

SECTION XXXVII.

BIRTH AND DEATH.

In days of old when Buddha was residing in the Jetavana Vihâra, near Śrâvastî, preaching his law[1] for the sake of Devas and men, there was a certain rich householder, a Brahman, who had a son just twenty years old, who had recently married a wife. And now seven days had passed after the marriage, when the young pair agreed to go together to the after-garden to look at the beautiful trees and flowers. It was just the third month of spring-time when they sallied forth. Amongst the other trees there was one beautiful plum-tree in blossom, the flowers of which were beyond their reach, but yet the bride longed to have one. On this the young man assayed to climb the tree to get his love a flower. Having reached a top-most branch, lo! it gave way beneath his weight, and he fell to the ground and was killed. Then there was great lamentation among the members of his family. The wails and cries of his friends resounded on every side—and after returning from his funeral obsequies—which were conducted according to the rules of religion—the house was again filled with the sounds of grief and lamentation. On this the World-honoured, perceiving the circumstances of the case, came at once to the dwelling. On seeing him, the father and mother and all the rest went forth and did him reverence; and on explaining the cause of their grief the master addressed the householder and said, "Cease

[1] The expression used here for "law," implies "the expanded law," or "saddharma."

your lamentations, and listen to me! All things around you are inconstant and destined to change! Once born, then there is death. Sin and its consequences are necessarily bound up together. And who is this youth, and who his relations for whom ye weep so pitifully and without intermission?" And then the Master repeated these verses:—

"What is life but the flower or the fruit which falls, when ripe, but yet which ever fears the untimely frost? Once born there is nought but sorrow; for who is there can escape death? From the first moment of conception in the womb, the result of passionate love and desire, there is nought but the bodily form, transitory as the lightning flash. It is difficult to dam up the daily flow of the waters of life. The body is but a thing destined to perish. There is no certain form given to the spirit conceived with the body. Once dead it is again born—the connections of sin and of merit cannot be overreached. It is not a matter of one life, or one death, but from the act of renewed conception proceeds all the consequences of former deeds, resulting in joy or misery; the body dies but the spirit is not entombed!"

After these verses were said, Buddha explained that the cause of the untimely death of the young bridegroom was, that in former days he had ruthlessly shot a young sparrow through the body, as he wandered through the garden of his house with three companions; and then after explaining the consequences of this proceeding in each case the World-honoured added these verses:

"It is the mind alone (spirit) that determines

the character of (life in) the three worlds. Just as the life has been virtuous or the contrary, is the subsequent career of the individual. Living in the dark, darkness will follow; the consequent birth is as the echo from the cavern, immersed in carnal desires, there cannot be any thing but carnal appetite; all things result from previous conduct, as the traces follow the elephant-step, or the shadow the substance."

After hearing these words, the householder and those who accompanied him were filled with joy, and accepted the terms of discipleship, and finally entered the Paths.

SECTION XXXVIII.

THE PROFIT OF RELIGION.

1. THERE was in former days a certain King who ruled his people justly, and with an earnest desire for their good; but he had no son to succeed him. Buddha, having come to his kingdom, he went to hear him preach, and being convinced of the truth he became a disciple. After this he ceased not to pray earnestly for a son. Now he had a little servant boy (keih-shi?) about eleven years old, who also devoted himself to religious exercises and the repetition of Scripture. This boy having died, was re-incarnated as a child of the King his master, and when he had arrived at the age of fifteen years he was publicly acknowledged as the Prince Royal (Kumâra). After a while, the King having died, the Prince ascended the throne, and he soon gave way to evil habits of self-indulgence, and the people and the kingdom suffered in consequence. On this Buddha, knowing all the circumstances of the case, once more visited the kingdom, and the Râja having gone to meet him, paid the usual obeisance. Buddha then began to explain to the King how it was he had come to his present royal dignity—viz., by his attention in former births to the five religious duties of a Shaman, which are these—1st, charity; 2d, founding religious buildings; 3d, reverence in worship; 4th, patience and self-restraint; 5th, diligent search after truth. By observing these he had attained his present rank; and then the World-honoured added these words, and said:—

"A man who knows how to reverence the higher powers, his parents, and religious teachers—who is full of faith, and obedience, and charity, and wisdom—shall certainly in the end attain a fortunate condition of birth. His destiny being thus a felicitous one, if born in the world he will be a ruler of men[1] ("prince," or "honourable," among men), and by his wisdom will be able to control the empire. Reverencing the law, it cannot be but that he will become lord of men. And so continuing in the path of virtue, and not receding therefrom, he will ever be so born, and without any intermission enjoy increasing happiness."

Buddha having thus spoken, explained how the King had come to his present dignity, and urged him not to give way, now he had attained such a position, to the temptations of sense, and then added these lines:—

"The man who possesses authority in the world, practising himself in right dealing, and not using violence, regulating his thoughts, and overcoming all wicked desires, thus becomes a king of the law (or a righteous king). Seeing that which is right, he is able to do good; loving virtue, he is able to profit men; and thus, by an impartiality of conduct, he treats all and makes all, as it were, his own equals and fellows."

The King having heard these words, was filled with penitence, and bowing down at Buddha's feet, he received the five rules of a lay disciple, and entered the first Path.

2. In days of old, when Buddha was residing at the Jetavana Vihára, near Śrâvastî, preaching his law for the good

[1] Compare the Greek ἄναξ ἀνδρων (*Juventus Mundi*, cap. vi.).

of Devas and men, at this time there was in a country some way to the south a very large elephant of a threefold colour, white, blue, and black, which the King very much desired to capture and to tame, so as to make it one of his fighting elephants. Accordingly having despatched his chief hunter for the purpose, he waited in expectation of his command being obeyed. Now there was at this time in the mountains a certain divine elephant, his body white as snow, his tail red as vermilion, and his tusks yellow as gold. Having seen this creature, the hunter returned to the King, and asked him whether the elephant he had been sent to capture was of this kind. The King immediately ordered the beast to be taken and brought to him. On this the hunter, with thirty men, went in pursuit of him. Having come to the spot, and surrounded the place, the elephant, knowing their purpose, allowed the men to approach him, and then, filled with fury, he rushed at them and trampled the nearest to death, and put the others to flight. Now at this time in the side of the mountain there was a young and lusty hermit, who had long practised his religious austerities without arriving at any degree of fixedness. Seeing from a distance the sad case of these hunters, and pitying their condition, relying on his strength, he hurried to the spot, hoping to save them. Meantime Buddha, seeing the danger of this Bhikshu, and fearing lest the divine elephant should kill him, quickly transported himself to the place, and standing beside the elephant, caused the glory of his person to exhibit itself. The elephant, seeing the brilliancy of the body of Buddha, appeased his rage, and gave up the pursuit of the men. The Bhikshu also seeing the wonderful light that shone forth, bowed down at Buddha's feet, who forthwith repeated these verses:—

"Be not so foolishly angry with the divine elephant as thus to entangle yourself in the certain calamity that will follow your conduct; the evil thought produces self-destruction, and in the end accomplishes no good."

The Bhikshu, having heard these words, was convinced that he was wrong in giving loose to the thoughts he had, and in deep penitence bowing at Buddha's feet, obtained wisdom.

[The next story is that of Buddha, in a similar way to the last, converting a Raksha, who had attacked a city to the south of Râjagriha, and devoured many of its inhabitants; on which occasion the Master recited these lines:—

"One who is able to rely upon the saving power of virtue (virtuous, or moral conduct), a happy destiny ever follows that man, and by perception of religious truth (the law) he becomes conspicuous among his fellow-men. And thus he finally escapes the three evil modes of birth; getting rid of anger by strict moral government, he also drives away sorrow and fear; he rises to be chief of the three worlds (Buddha); then neither Nâgas or demons, or noxious, poisonous snakes, can hurt *him*, the man who disobeys not the laws of virtuous conduct."]

[The next story relates to Buddha when he was in a former birth a chakravarttin (universal monarch), and made a rule that he and his descendants should give up their empire and become Shamans on the appearance of the first white hair on their heads (a similar story is found in the "previous history" of Buddha, in the "Romantic Legend," pp. 18, 19)].

SECTION XXXIX.

GOOD FORTUNE (MAHÁMANGALA).[1]

WHEN Buddha was residing in the Gridhrakûta Mountain, near Râjagriha, preaching for the benefit of Devas and men, there was residing on the banks of the Ganges a certain Brahmachârin, belonging to the Nirgrantha sect, of considerable age and vast wisdom. This man, with his 500 followers, devoted himself to the study of the stars and heavenly bodies, with a view to predict lucky and unlucky events. On one occasion, just before Buddha had commenced his public ministry, this man, with his disciples, were discussing the question of "good fortune," as they sat by the river's side; and after explaining in what good fortune consisted, so far as it concerned the happiness of a prince in his worldly empire, the question arose as to what "good fortune" was when considered in reference to the future. After much discussion, they resolved to go to the Bôdhi Tree, where the World-honoured had just overcome Mâra, and put this question to him, What is the secret of real "good fortune"? On which the Master opened his mouth and repeated these lines:—

"Buddha, the Honoured above all gods, Tathâgata, the ever-wise and intelligent, is asked by the learned sages of the Brahmachârin sect in what consists the enjoyment of good fortune. On this Buddha, the compassionate, for their sake enunciates true wisdom. He who has faith, and de-

[1] This section agrees with the "Mahámangala Sutta" of the Sutta Nipâta.

lights in the true Law, this man is fortunate above all others. He who looks for good luck neither from gods or sacrifices to spirits (but from himself) is truly fortunate. A friend of the virtuous, and holding with the righteous, always making the consideration of virtue his first aim, keeping his body in strict obedience to the rules of propriety, this man is fortunate indeed! Avoiding bad people and following the good, giving up wine, and using strict moderation in all personal gratification, not lusting after female beauty, this man is indeed a fortunate one. Ever anxious to listen to the rules of right conduct, persevering in the study of the Law and Rules of Discipline (Dharma and Vinaya), self-restrained and without offence, this man is fortunate above all. If a householder, then caring for his father and mother, and looking after the welfare of his house, and properly fostering his wife and child, not occupying himself in vain and useless avocations, this man is indeed fortunate. Not giving way to idleness or self-honour, knowing the character of moderation (as to himself), and thoughtful of his friends, at proper times reading the Scriptures and practising (himself in them), this man is truly fortunate. Patiently continuing in the way of duty (of what he hears he ought to do), rejoicing to see a religious person (Shaman), and ever inviting such an one to instruct him in religion, this man is happy. Observing the religious seasons (fasts), and during such seasons using strict self-abstinence, always desiring to see the virtuous and holy man, placing his confidence in the instruction of the enlightened, this man is fortunate. Once convinced of the happiness of religion (Bôdhi), then with upright heart never swerving from his faith, desiring above all things to escape the three evil ways (of birth), this man is truly happy. With equal mind, devoting himself to charity, honouring all the wise alike, and paying respect to the Divine Spirits, this man is indeed happy. Always anxious to get rid of sensual desires and covetousness, to escape from delusive thoughts, ignorance, and anger, ever constant in the pursuit of true wisdom, this man is indeed fortunate. Even in discarding the evil using no extraordinary appearance of effort, but steadily persevering in the practice of what is right, always acting as he ought to act, this man is fortunate indeed. Full of love for all things in the world, practising virtue in order to benefit others, this man alone is happy. The wise man dwelling in the world, pursuing this line of fortunate behaviour with constancy, ever pressing onwards to complete what knowledge he has gained, this is a happy man indeed."

The Brahmachârin, having heard the instruction of Buddha, felt his heart full of joy; immediately he arose and worshipped, and took refuge in Buddha, the Law, and the Church.

The Nirgrantha and his followers, having heard these words, were very glad, and after due worship they obtained permission to become Shamans, and soon obtained inward illumination (the eyes of the Law).